STUDENT

FREEDOM

REVISITED

Contemporary Issues & Perspectives

Editors
Robert L. Ackerman
William B. Werner
Louis C. Vaccaro

NASPA
Student Affairs Administrators
in Higher Education

Additional copies may be purchased by contacting the NASPA publications department at 301-638-1749 or visiting http://www.naspa.org/publications.

ISBN 0-931654-34-3

Table of Contents

About the Authors. v

Foreword. xi
    Jerry H. Gill

Editors' Introduction. xv
    Robert L. Ackerman, William B. Werner, and Louis C. Vaccaro

Chapter 1.   Student Academic Freedom: An Uncertain Future. 1
                Robert L. Ackerman

Chapter 2.   Student Activism: A View from an Administrator. 15
                Keith M. Miser

Chapter 3.   Campus Subcultures and the Emergence of
                Student Freedom in American Higher Education. 29
                Louis C. Vaccaro

Chapter 4.   Diversity and Student Freedom. 39
                Corlisse D. Thomas and André McKenzie

Chapter 5.   International Dimensions of Student Freedom. 55
                Sabine U. O'Hara

Chapter 6.   Contemporary Issues in the Constitutional Rights of
                Students in American Higher Education. 65
                William B. Werner

Chapter 7.   Working in the Wake of the Sexual Revolution. 79
                Holly Hippensteel

Chapter 8.   Freedom, But for What?. 87
                Rev. Christopher DeGiovine

Chapter 9.   Student Financial Freedom. 97
                Kevin Kucera

Chapter 10. The Impact of Educational Innovation on
Student Freedom: The Case of Distance Education
in Higher Education 103
Lenoar Foster

Chapter 11. The Political Involvement of Students 115
Aaron Kreider

Chapter 12. Student Activism Today......................... 127
Seth Kujat

Chapter 13. Student Governance and Leadership................ 135
Emily A. Langdon

About the Authors

Robert L. Ackerman

Since 2000, Robert L. Ackerman has been associate professor of higher education and coordinator of graduate studies in the Department of Educational Leadership at the University of Nevada, Las Vegas (UNLV). Prior to that appointment, he served for 29 years as a student affairs administrator at three campuses, including 11 years as the vice president and dean of students at Saint Leo College in Florida and 14 years as the vice president for student affairs at UNLV. Ackerman served on the *NASPA Journal* editorial board and has published numerous articles within the journal. He received his doctorate from Indiana University and his research interests include mentoring for professionals, the history of higher education and higher education finance.

Rev. Christopher DeGiovine

Rev. Christopher DeGiovine is an ordained Roman Catholic priest of the Diocese of Albany, New York. Ordained for 27 years, Rev. DeGiovine has been dean of spiritual life and chaplain at the College of Saint Rose in Albany, NY for the past 15 years. In that capacity, Rev. DeGiovine works with the entire college community on issues relating to the mission and heritage of the college and to the spiritual and religious development of the college community. Rev. DeGiovine is also an adjunct faculty member at the college and at St. Bernard's Institute of Theology in Albany. Rev. DeGiovine holds a Doctor of Ministry from The Catholic University of America in Washington, DC.

Lenoar Foster

Lenoar Foster is an associate professor of Educational Leadership and Higher Education in the College of Education at Washington State University, Pullman, where he serves as the program coordinator for graduate degree programs in higher education. He received his doctorate in Educational Administration and Higher Education from the University of Nevada, Reno. Prior to coming to Washington State University he served as a tenured faculty member of the educational leadership faculties at the University of Montana and San Diego State University. He lectures nationally and internationally on distance education while his research interests span a wide range of higher education issues. Among his publications is *Distance Education: Teaching and Learning in Higher Education* (with Beverly L. Bower and Lemuel Watson, 2002, Boston: Pearson Custom Publishing).

Jerry H. Gill

Jerry H. Gill received his master's degree in Philosophy from the University of Washington and his PhD from Duke University. He has taught at a number of small colleges around the country, the most recent being The College of Saint Rose in Albany, NY. Currently he is academic coordinator for BorderLinks, an organization providing experiential education opportunities on the U.S./Mexico border. He has also published many books and journal articles in the fields of religion, philosophy, and education.

Holly Hippensteel

Holly Hippensteel is the coordinator for community standards at Carnegie Mellon University in Pittsburgh, PA. Holly received her Master of Arts degree in Student Affairs in Higher Education from Indiana University of Pennsylvania after completing her undergraduate work in Sociology at La Roche College. She has served as a student affairs practitioner in various capacities for nearly a decade.

Aaron Kreider

Aaron Kreider is an online activist and anarchist who lives in Philadelphia. He currently works on an interactive website for progressive campus activists: http://www.CampusActivism.org. While working on a master's degree in Sociology at Notre Dame, he founded the Progressive Student Alliance. The group fought hard for LGBT rights on campus (but lost) and won its antisweatshop campaign. He has written for *Z Magazine* and the *Student Environmental Action Coalition Organizing Guide*.

Kevin Kucera

With nearly 25 years of higher education experience at three catholic institutions, Kevin Kucera is presently serving as dean of admissions and enrollment services at Siena Heights University (MI). Kevin comes from a strong financial aid background having served over 10 years as a financial aid director, and was elected president of the Wisconsin Association of Financial

Aid Administrators in 1996. Mr. Kucera is a frequent lecturer at higher education conferences describing strategies to create "customized recruitment plans," utilizing research-driven data, to communicate effective messages to prospective students.

Seth Kujat

Seth Kujat is a senior at Kent State University studying Communication Studies and Applied Conflict Management. He was an undergraduate student senator and president of the May 4th Task force. While on undergraduate student senate, he petitioned a referendum to establish permanent funding for the annual May 4th Commemoration, which ultimately passed and put into effect at the end of his term. Mr. Kujat is also president and a founding father of Lambda Chi Alpha fraternity at Kent State University.

Emily A. Langdon

Emily A. Langdon received a BA in International Relations from the University of California, Davis; an MEd with a specialization in College student personnel administration from Colorado State University; and a PhD in Higher Education and Organizational Change from UCLA. While at UCLA, she worked at the Higher Education Research Institute on a federally funded Eisenhower grant creating the Social Change Model of Leadership Development. Langdon has worked in various student affairs and leadership development positions, and published research on women's colleges in *The Peabody Journal of Education* and *New Directions for Institutional Research*. She is currently a senior consultant at Performa, Inc., a firm that focuses on planning, organizational development, and facilities design for private higher education.

André McKenzie

André McKenzie is vice president for academic support services at St. John's University (NY). In his over 20 years as a higher education administrator, McKenzie has served in various student affairs and academic affairs positions. In addition to his current administrative duties, McKenzie serves as an adjunct assistant professor on both the undergraduate and graduate levels. An author and coauthor of articles appearing in the *NASPA Journal*, he is also a contributing author to the recently published *African-American*

Fraternities and Sororities: The Legacy and the Vision. McKenzie earned his Doctor of Education and Master of Education degrees from Teachers College, Columbia University. He received his Master of Science and Bachelor of Science degrees from Illinois State University.

Keith M. Miser

Keith M. Miser served as a chief student affairs officer for 29 years before coming to the University of Hawaii at Hilo to serve as the vice chancellor for student affairs. He has served on the editorial board for the *Journal of College Student Development,* and as the editor of the *NASPA Journal.* He has held numerous positions of leadership in professional organizations including U.S. cochair of the Consortium for Belize Educational Cooperation and member of the board of directors of the NASPA Foundation. He has also given more than 70 presentations at national and regional conferences and published 20 articles or chapters in professional literature in higher education. Dr. Miser is a native of Indiana and holds his Bachelor of Science in Biology, Master of Science in Counseling and Guidance, and Doctor of Education in Higher Education, all from the Indiana University College of Education.

Sabine U. O'Hara

Sabine U. O'Hara, president of Roanoke College in Salem, VA, is a well-known researcher and author in ecological economics, sustainable community development, and economics and ethics. In addition, she has been active in developing innovative models for teaching economics. Her publications include two books, more than 30 peer-reviewed articles and book chapters, and numerous popular publications and research reports. She has lectured widely in the United States, Latin and Central America, and Europe, including her native Germany. She serves on the editorial board of the *Review of Social Economy* and as a board member of the Association of Social Economics. She received her doctorate in Environmental Economics from the University of Goettingen, and has held both academic and administrative positions, including director of public policy for the NYS Council of Churches.

Corlisse D. Thomas

Corlisse D. Thomas is currently associate dean of student affairs at Columbia University. For more than 15 years she has held a variety of student affairs positions. She cowrote, "Cultural Dynamics and Issues in Higher Education," a chapter in *Addressing Cultural Issues in Organizations*, and "Pre-Collegiate Experiences, Values, and Goals of First-Year Students of Color," a chapter in the most recent edition of the *First Year Experience Monograph Series*. Her research interests include the experiences of students of color within higher education and the impact of popular culture on student values. Thomas received both her master's and doctoral degrees in Higher Education from Teachers College, Columbia University.

Louis C. Vaccaro

Louis C. Vaccaro has served as president of several colleges and in a variety of administrative and faculty positions since earning his Bachelor of Arts in Economics and Social Sciences and Master of Arts from the University of Southern California, completing a second master's degree at California State University in Northridge, and finishing his doctorate in Higher Education and Sociology at Michigan State University. The author and editor of six books and nearly 100 articles and book reviews, Dr. Vaccaro has excelled from the mid-1970s through the turn of the century as an international lecturer and consultant. Dr. Vaccaro has received numerous awards and honors, and held prestigious positions, the most recent in February and March of 2004 when Dr. Vaccaro was the Fulbright senior specialist in Honduras at the Universidad Pedagogica Nacional Francisco Morazon (UPNFM).

William B. Werner

William B. Werner is an attorney at law, assistant professor in the William F. Harrah College of Hotel Administration at the University of Nevada, Las Vegas (UNLV), and an adjunct faculty member in the William S. Boyd School of Law at UNLV. Prior to his current appointment in 2001, he was associate general counsel for Boyd Gaming Corporation in Las Vegas. He serves as editor of several hospitality and tourism journals and publishes primarily in the areas of hospitality, employment, and gaming law.

Foreword

Jerry H. Gill

It is an honor to write the foreword to this significant collection of essays. As one who has been directly involved in higher education, both as a student and as a professor, for over 50 years, I can honestly say that I have learned a great deal from reading this book. The authors of these essays provide an excellent review of the issues and developments revolving around the notion of student freedom over the past quarter of a century.

I have always been enamored of the definition of the term *freedom* attributed to Robert Frost: "Freedom is moving easy in harness." Among other things, this definition suggests that there are always parameters within which the idea and practice of freedom must operate, and that is the theme I wish to explore in these brief remarks.

In one way or another nearly all of the essays touch on two related issues—student freedom and student activism—as they surfaced in the late 1960s and early 1970s. The chief causes of this activism were the civil rights movement and a growing public dissatisfaction with the on-going Vietnam War. An ancillary cause was general student unhappiness with the impersonal and seemingly irrelevant character of many educational policies and results. This activism, in turn, triggered deeper and more general questions about the role of students in relation to the overall educational process itself.

And, while this may not be the place to summarize or analyze the contents of this collection of highly stimulating essays, it is the place to encourage readers to engage these writers and issues directly, for they focus on and explore many diverse aspects of an extremely important topic. In addition, this is also the place to offer a few brief reflections of my own on the concept of freedom, especially as it relates to the dynamics of contemporary higher education. Hopefully my remarks will enrich the mix of ideas advanced by the authors of the ensuing chapters.

My own thinking about these matters has been strongly influenced by the insights of the philosopher Michael Polanyi, especially as they are expressed in his books *Personal Knowledge: Toward a Postcritical Philosophy, and Knowing and Being*. These insights are especially relevant to postmodern education, and nearly every essay in this volume acknowledges the challenges to both education and freedom presented by postmodern thought.

Three key issues surrounding postmodernism are critical to the future of student freedom. First, all efforts to communicate, postmodernist efforts included, clearly entail the tacit assumption that understanding and agreement are both possible and desirable. In other words, people talk in order to communicate, trusting that others will not only listen but will respond, and perhaps even agree. Polanyi (1964) calls this character of speech "universal intent" (p. 309), and offers it as a *sine qua non* of all human language. While postmodernists maintain that all language is relative and subject to alternative interpretations, not all interpretations are equally viable, nor are all contexts and agendas indiscernible. In this context, student activism and protest must be seen not just as an act of defiance but also as an attempt to be understood and to gain support from others.

Second, and similarly, with respect to the concept of freedom itself, it should be clear that both the notion and the practice of freedom are parasitic on tradition and convention. Without an initial, if unspoken, acknowledgement of parental, pedagogical, and political authority, there can be no cultural life at all, let alone any possibility of and concern for individual freedom. Polanyi (1969) makes this point by insisting that social agreement and mutual commitment are "logically prior" (p. 173) to individuality and freedom.

This point is akin to that made by those who insist that our individual selves initially arise out of a social context, that the "self" seeking freedom is indeed a "social self." Thus freedom, even and perhaps especially educational freedom, can only function within social parameters. In response to Pink Floyd's cry for freedom in the album *The Wall*, "We don't need no education; We don't need no thought control" (Waters & Gilmour, 1979), a friend of mine once remarked in a commencement address, "If you do not want mind control, you had better be sure to get an education" (R. Hollowell, Spokane Falls Community College commencement address, 1980).

Third, many of the essays in this volume stress the need for a common cultural or core value commitment that can guide us through the maze of multicultural, postmodern, and technological challenges with which the idea of freedom is confronted today. I am not particularly optimistic about our chances of finding a basis for such unity, but if it is to be found, it can only be the result of honest and on-going dialogue among those within what Polanyi (1969) labels the "society of explorers" (p. 65). Let's keep the conversation going.

In her album *Speed of Light*, Holly Near warns, "We are the sailors of this ship, but we are in mutiny. The future of this journey depends on unity" (1982). She goes on to suggest that we must set our differences aside and "make way for the speed of light," the only absolute in a universe of relativity. She takes this absolute to be a "unity" of commitment that will serve as the axis around which our common concerns and disagreements can orbit. The authors of these essays surely agree!

References

Near, H. (1982). *Speed of light*. Ukiah, CA: Redwood Records.

Polanyi, M. (1964). *Personal knowledge: Toward a postcritical philosophy*. New York: Harper and Row.

Polanyi, M. (1969). *Knowing and being*. Chicago: University of Chicago Press

Waters, R. & Gilmour, D. (1979). Another brick in the wall, part 2 [Recorded by Pink Floyd]. On *The wall* [CD]. New York: Columbia Records.

Editors' Introduction

Robert L. Ackerman, William B. Werner, and Louis C. Vaccaro

During the late 1960s and early '70s, a powerful new force appeared on the campuses of America's colleges and universities. That force, usually referred to as "student activism," was felt in varying degrees in some large universities and smaller colleges from coast to coast and its effects and consequences are still felt in many ways today. Indeed, many present-day campus policies, programs, and practices originated, or at least changed drastically, in response to the students' new social and political activism and their battle for personal freedom and civil rights during that turbulent time. Moreover, many of the student activists of that period are university faculty and administrators today.

Almost immediately from the beginning of the Berkeley free speech movement, a rash of books, articles, and scholarly papers emerged to explain the causes, reasons, and consequences of the new phenomenon known as student activism. The explanations, analyses, and descriptions of this campus "unrest" and of the concept of student "freedom" were as varied as the backgrounds of authors. One such book, published at the height of campus disturbances in 1969 by Teachers College Press, was *Student Freedom in American Higher Education* (Vaccaro & Covert). Its editors, a professor of history and the academic vice-president at the University of Portland, brought together 12 faculty, students, and administrators to attempt to identify and address some of the salient issues implicit in student activism and the movement for student freedom.

As might be expected, there was little unanimity in the discourse. Indeed, as Jacquelyn Grennan, then president of Webster College, observed in her foreword to the book, "The value judgments within this area represented by the authors of these essays display, on a kind of 'mini-scale', the same kind of range, difference, and even polarity of view which, I believe, characterizes the dissenters themselves" (Vaccaro & Covert, 1969, p. iii). Despite the lack of agreement among the authors, however, the book provided a broad foundation for the discovery and analysis of the new issues facing American university students, faculty, and administrators, from emerging student legal rights, political causes, and subcultures to the role of students in shaping university, social, and political policy.

This volume brings together a different, but equally diverse group of scholars, administrators, professionals, and students, and, likewise, divergent views and opinions. As in the original volume, the authors and, ultimately, the reader, are asked to consider the origins, development, causes, and potential consequences of various issues attendant to the topic of student freedom. This book was not intended merely to update the 1969 essays, although the authors of this volume were free to do so. Rather, the purpose of this book is to build upon that foundation—to identify, describe, and analyze the current state of student freedom in American higher education and the various issues posed by the topic, both new and old.

If there is a common conclusion that may be drawn from the chapters in this volume, it is that the question of student freedom is no less relevant or critical today than it was in 1969. Having won recognition and legal support for academic and social freedoms long denied them, today's college students are left to defend them, and to wonder where to go next. If the old value system of higher education was effectively abolished in the early 1970s, then what has replaced it?

Student activism, likewise, may receive much less press attention than in earlier years but is no less a part of college life today. Frances Cox Piven of New York University recently proclaimed in a forum entitled "Liberalism Regained: Building the next progressive majority":

> We've also seen the universities come alive, and not just over Iraq. A few years ago it was the living-wage campaigns for university employees, and before that the anti-sweatshop campaigns. Fifteen years ago, as I went from one university to another, nobody was really interested in economic issues. Today they are definitely interested . . . It's quite a change. ("Liberalism Regained," 2004, p. 32)

The two chapters by current student activists provide uncommon insight into this resurgence of campus activism. Other chapters focus on the dominant themes in student freedom today, from technology, politics, and finances to diversity, sex, and law. Although omissions are inevitable, the editors' intent was to identify these dominant themes and for each one to present the views of a scholar with particular knowledge and/or experience relating to it.

We realize and in fact hope that some who read this volume will have experienced for themselves some aspects the 1969 activism and unrest on American campuses. Those readers, like some of the authors in this volume, may find that they have a very different view of student freedom than they did thirty years ago. Younger readers, particularly current students, may find both surprise and amusement at the antics of their predecessors as well as an understanding of the origins and meanings of the freedom they enjoy on campus today. To be sure, this volume raises more questions that it resolves, but whatever the reader's particular interest in higher education, he or she will find in these pages both diverse perspectives and valuable analysis of the modern and emerging issues in student freedom.

Whatever the reader's reaction, it is our hope that this collection of essays will provide not only an update on the status of student freedom and activism but also a fresh perspective from which to analyze student freedom and activism and their value to American higher education and society.

References

Liberalism regained: Building the next progressive majority. (2004, August). *Harper's Magazine*, 309(1851), 31-38.

Vaccaro, L.C. & Covert, J. T. (Eds.). (1969). *Student freedom in American higher education*. Columbia, NY: Teachers College Press.

Chapter 1

Student Academic Freedom: An Uncertain Future

Robert L. Ackerman

> Students are part of the educational process, contributors to it and not merely beneficiaries of it. They do as much to educate one another as teachers do, and sometimes they educate teachers. The freedom of the academic community, therefore rightly includes the freedom of students to continue inquiry and debate outside the classroom. (Frankel, 1966, p. 242)

Academic freedom, like so many aspects of American higher education, was not born in the United States but it has been nurtured in this country. The concept of academic freedom, *lehrfreiheit*, the freedom to teach, was brought to the United States by those late 19th century American scholars who studied in Germany. The freedom to teach has become a cherished linchpin of scholarship, the right of a college or university faculty member to pursue truth, to conduct research, and to teach free from interference. Academic freedom fits well with the concept of free speech, another ideal that in order to work needs to be protected and defended.

The companion concept that existed in Germany and could also have come back with those early faculty members, returning with newly minted PhDs and a respect for unfettered scholarship, is *lernfreiheit*, the freedom students had to learn. As practiced in Germany, *lernfreiheit* permitted students to move from university to university to study topics of interest. Perhaps it was because the freedom to teach does not depend on freedom to learn, but *lernfreiheit* did not transplant to the United States. There were no leaders within the academy to implement it, no idealists to nurture and protect it. Freedom to learn, when it did sprout in the United States, did so around issues such as the elective curriculum, a slowly evolving process that gave students increasing choice in what they would study. The history of American higher education records accounts of the fights over freedom to teach, a protection faculty had to win. And, win it they did, securing for faculty unique-to-the-profession freedoms. Time would pass before students would gain freedoms in the form of limited control over what they would study and how.

Universities may have been enlightened places, although one could hardly tell that by reviewing the student conduct codes that existed before the mid 1960s. From their very beginnings, colleges and universities in the United States exercised control over students. Those early students did not so much go to college as they were sent and, in the sending, the students' parents had expectations. In loco parentis, the concept that the institution acted in place of the parents, was very much part of campus life even as Harvard College was organized more than a hundred years before the Revolutionary War. The food would get better, some student conduct rules were relaxed, and socially acceptable outlets were found, but rules governing many aspects of student life remained in place until protesting students made institutional control over their lives an issue in the middle part of the 20th century, at a time when signing out to leave campus was still required, particularly of women students (Rudolph, 1990, p. 102).

The 1960s marked an era in American higher education that will forever be known for student-led protests and general campus unrest. It can be argued that those campus protests were not only about students gaining control of campus life but, whatever the various motivations, students gained freedoms and passed those on to succeeding generations. Campus life as it exists today was shaped by those students who took to the barricades in protest of an unpopular war, the absence of minorities on campus, an often uncaring but always bureaucratic multiversity, and a long tradition of administrative control over the lives of students. Protesting students carried signs with messages like "I am a human being. Please do not fold, spindle or mutilate me," expressing commonly held frustrations. Students did not feel that they were being well-served by social institutions, including colleges and universities. Student personnel administrators accepted responsibility for the well-being of students by controlling their lives, but that responsibility ended when the protests began. If the campus unrest that marked the era, the 1960s, resulted in the death of the institution as parent, a demise that was mourned by some, it also resulted in an increased concern by students for social issues. Once control was loosened, students turned their interests elsewhere while college administrators scurried to keep up.

Throughout the history of higher education there are examples of students who, fed up with the lack of responsiveness from college leadership, developed programs that circumvented the institution while meeting student needs. Students have always protested. Sometimes student unrest was the expression of boredom, other times because there was an "administrator who exercised discretion without legitimacy" (Mayhew, 1969, p. 59). It is noteworthy that student unrest worked, it resulted in change and often that change was long lasting. Early colleges offered a proscribed curriculum, a specified set of courses having very little to do with the experiences of students or the skills needed to meet the challenges faced by those who would build a nation. Following a liberal arts curriculum that had its beginnings in the middle ages and using Greek and Latin, the ancient languages, in an environment more interested in control and order than in scholarship and learning was, for most, a boring, meaningless experience. Students found creative outlets for their considerable energy and, in a very real sense, exercised the freedom to learn before faculty began to attach any importance to the freedom to teach. Protests, many of which were violent, were frequent, reflecting the hostility that existed between the colleges and their students. Student clubs and organizations—fraternities, literary societies, debating clubs, and athletic competitions—all had their beginnings as students looked beyond the classroom to pursue things that interested them. Jefferson at Virginia proposed a student government; had the concept been implemented at his institution or been adopted on other campuses, it might have provided the vehicle through which students could have exercised greater freedoms. But organized input from students into institutional decision making was still off in the future.

What students developed were opportunities to learn. It would take some time for these initiatives to be recognized as creating learning environments, and the concept that student involvement was to be valued for the contributions it made to the process of education was still a long time away from being accepted. Of course, many of the programs that were built would eventually become part of institutionalized administrative structures and students, the ones who had the ideas and who did the start up work, would no longer be in charge. Administrators would be appointed to direct these programs, giving rise to the student personnel profession, as well as to athletic departments. Unable to change the proscribed curriculum, students looked elsewhere and used their creative energies to fill a void. From time to time there were objections to these student initiatives; frequently those objections were based on the secret culture and boorish behavior of fraternity members. But for the most part, faculty and administrators, occupied as they were with other issues, ignored students; left to themselves, students constructed an extra-curriculum that essentially shaped college life and expanded the concept of learning by removing it from the structure of the classroom.

The classical curriculum that came to American higher education from England would eventually give way to some student choice. Not quite *lernfreiheit*, but curriculum choice did give students some freedom to determine what they would learn, at least in terms of the classes they would take. At the minimum, students could express likes or dislikes by selecting one class over another, one professor over another, or one course of study over some other. As more colleges were founded, students had some choice as to where to attend. Having choices of what to study and where to study would become for students a form of academic freedom. As it was developing in the early 19th century, no one imagined the impact that giving students choices would have on the character of higher education; nor was it known how students would exercise these freedoms. But institutional sensitivity to the ability of students to move from campus to campus and within a campus among the various academic programs, now very much part of the fabric of American higher education, has greatly impacted colleges and universities as they now compete for students. Within colleges, academic programs compete for students as students exercise the freedom they have to make choices about what and with whom they will study.

Going to college and engaging in serious academic work once they got there was not something students took seriously until the influx of returning military veterans following World War II (WWII). Student life outside the classroom was both more interesting and more important for students than was scholarship, as the extra-curriculum became the central educational experience. Faculty busied themselves developing academic specializations. Faculty scholarship in the form of research was beginning to take hold; being a professor was becoming a profession, not as it once had been, something to do until called to a pulpit. As scholarship become important to faculty so did the protections of academic freedom and tenure, the full exercise of *lehrfreiheit*. Faculty-led movements fought for and gained those protections and, while the hold of faculty over the academy began to take form, students remained uninvolved and little interested. Enrollments grew as access to college became a national issue but, for the most part, students focused on college life and social pursuits, expressing little concern for academic freedom in any form.

There were efforts to merge the activities of the classroom with those of the extra-curriculum, and student governments were beginning to take form. The focus of these earliest forms of student participation was not institutional decision making, but on student discipline and activities management. In an effort to build partnerships, some students were invited to serve on some committees and student leaders were able to make contact with administrators. While still not as important to most students as was the fun of the extra-curriculum, increasingly students began to focus attention what was happening inside of the classroom. Some of the social and political debates that engaged the external community found their way to college campuses as students in at least limited numbers became activists (Cohen, 1998, pp. 202-206).

The 1960s in the United States were a very difficult time. Social concerns marked the period, leading to unrest that would find its way to the campuses. The list of social issues was a long one that included a war in Southeast Asia that divided the country; a military draft that provided soldiers for that war; civil and equal rights agendas brought forward by long neglected Americans seeking a rightful place at the table; the assassinations of political and civil rights leaders that would challenge the nation's sense of stability; and, the bureaucratic treatment of students by campus administrators. (Feuer, 1969). The Mr. Chips ideal of the kindly professor had by then been replaced by the detached researcher, more at home in the lab than the classroom, more comfortable with fellow scientists than with students. Disenfranchised students merged political and social agendas to form a volatile mix. Higher education had developed to where it served the national interest and, because it did, the campuses became focal points of social protest. The student protest movements that marked this period did not occur on every campus or even a majority of the campuses, and on the campuses where they did occur, a majority of the students chose not to participate. However, the issues students confronted were important and the changes to the structure and operation of colleges and universities that resulted were significant. The culture of contentment that had defined campuses would change with the student protests of the 1960s.

Freedom, particularly academic freedom for students, was not an important issue in higher education in the United States, unlike in Europe where campus tensions ran high and disturbances were common. A 1964 survey of student freedoms (Williamson & Cowan, 1966) found that approximately 30% of university presidents did not support the statement that "an essential part of the education of each student is the freedom to hear, critically examine, and expresses viewpoints on a range of positions held and advocated regarding issues that divide society" (p. 257). (It should be noted that in 2004 at least two college or university presidents cancelled campus appearances by a controversial film maker, suggesting that students may not yet have gained the right to hear and examine differing points of view [Argetsinger, 2004; Petrillo, 2004]). An equally large percentage of presidents felt that the abolition of interracial marriage laws was a topic too controversial to be discussed on their campuses. If students had been docile, content to languish in the extracurriculum, the political and social turmoil that marked the late 1960s and early 1970s served to bring out other characteristics. Before the students took to the barricades in protest, student attitudes were marked by conformity, usually to the will of the faculty and institutional administration. That willingness to conform would be challenged by an intense involvement in social issues as students sought a voice in all matters of things of interest to them (Kunen, 1968; Maraniss, 2003).

A consistent thread throughout the history of American higher education has been student distain for the academic curriculum. The classical curriculum of an earlier time lacked meaning so students turned to the extra-curriculum. Following WWII when returning veterans brought a more serious tone to the campus, and when students had choices that would have been unimaginable even a short time before, the course of study was viewed as faculty-, not learner-centered, an obstacle to be overcome on the way to a degree and a career. That changed in the 1960s when, among the things that interested student protesters was the curriculum. Bloustein (1969), then president of Bennington College, observed that "students are growing impudent; sulking and unwilling to attend classes and take notes; they are protesting, striking, sitting in, demanding a voice in the governance of their colleges ... Students are seeking a new role in academic life" (p. 93). Demonstrating students demanded a voice in faculty hiring and evaluation, as well as an expansion of course offerings to include ethnic and women's studies and nonwestern literature and history. The faculty generally did not welcome students meddling in to their territory, protected as it was by the firmly entrenched freedom to teach. Students also focused attention on opening the opportunities of higher education to groups for whom college was not part of their American dream. Once again, faculty did not welcome this intrusion of students into what had been their sole province, determining who would be taught. The sentiment of the faculty is captured by van den Haag (1971) who noted that "concerning instruction in American universities, I have never heard a respectable argument for letting students influence what is to be taught, or by whom, or who is to be admitted" (p. 57). The prevailing attitude was that if students were unhappy with their courses, or with their professors, or with the university for whatever reason, they could leave to pursue other options, the love-it-or-leave-it solution. Faculty in general were not receptive to any freedom-to-learn claims made by students. Accommodation and collaboration were components of any definition of student-faculty relationship. Slowly campus leaders relented, providing opportunities for students to evaluate teaching, offering nonwestern culture courses, as well as women's and ethnic studies to the curriculum, and by implementing programs to enhance access by underrepresented populations (Slaughter, 2002). Students gained membership on faculty and institution-wide committees and began to have some voice in the management and administration of the campus beyond student life programs. Some colleges and universities found ways to include students among the voices present when boards of trustees set policy. These reforms marked significant progress in developing a semblance of academic freedoms as students began to influence what and how they learned. But including students in institutional decision making has not been accepted at all campuses, a point made by Boyer (1987):

> Student passivity is disturbing. Even more disturbing is the fact
> that most colleges in our study make too little effort to involve

students in governance on the campus ... We feel that
undergraduates should be encouraged not only to understand
how decisions are made at the college where they are enrolled,
but also they should be asked, indeed expected, to participate as
campus citizens as well. (p. 246)

The struggle to implement social change in higher education has been
prolonged and difficult. Similarly, colleges and universities did not willingly
give up paternalistic control over the lives of students even in the face of
social pressures to do so. It had always been that college students would have
fewer freedoms than would non-students, that students had to leave some
rights at the school door when they entered. The desire to gain freedom over
their personal lives motivated some of the student unrest and, while the
concept that students could be responsible for their personal affairs was
difficult to accept, colleges and universities did begin to change by modifying
conduct codes. In loco parentis, the guiding spirit of overprotective
administrators, had to be dismantled before there could be discussions of
other freedoms. Once that happened, students could more realistically
assume at least a modified role as partners in their own education.

The freedom of faculty to teach was debated and then reduced to writing,
agreed upon and adopted. Adoption had to include a mechanism for
enforcement. The American Association of University Professors (AAUP),
founded in 1915 and still a major force in higher education, was formed to
protect the academic freedoms central to the role of professor and the
intellectual life of the academy. The student movement of the 1960s resulted
in an increase in the academic freedoms of students and those changes, if
they were to become standard practice across higher education, had to be
debated and formally adopted. In 1967 five national organizations, including
the AAUP and the National Association of Student Personnel
Administrators (NASPA), framed a *Joint Statement on Rights and Freedoms of
Students*, a document that has been revisited and updated several times since
(AAUP, 1992). In its earliest form (*Student Bill of Rights*, 1967) the Joint
Statement, when viewed from the lens of the present, seems unnecessarily
restrictive and so the revisions, reflective of changing times, have been helpful.
One intent of the framers of the Joint Statement was to reunite the freedom
to teach and the freedom to learn, *lehrfreiheit* and *lernfreiheit*, as "inseparable
facets of academic freedom" (p. 1).

That the student in higher education is in a dependent relationship within the academy is clear from the tone of the Joint Statement. Students are reminded to exercise their freedoms with responsibility (p. 1), a caution that is a reoccurring theme throughout the document. Because the role of the student is as learner, proposed protections are not as detailed as they are for the faculty in their role as teacher. Within the document there is also a mixing of freedoms, some of which are constitutional in nature—the freedom of association is an example—with freedoms that are unique to the academy—such as freedom of inquiry. Students are not always able, with impunity, to "express their views on issues of institutional policy," as students are not always able, with impunity, "to invite and hear any person of their own choosing" (Argetsinger, 2004; Petrillo, 2004). Freedoms essential to learning and presumably protected by the Joint Statement have been challenged and, from time to time, abridged. Conflicts still occur over the content of student newspapers, an issue that has both constitutional and student academic freedom ramifications that the Joint Statement seeks to protect. In matters of student behavior, when their interests are involved, institutions can exercise special authority over incidents that occur off campus, a provision that may effectively limit the free exercise of the rights of citizenship. The debate regarding the extent to which standing as a student should impact other dimensions of an individual's life is not resolved by the Joint Statement although the conflict is imbedded in the folklore of higher education. As discussed elsewhere in this book, case law, including that dealing with speech codes, and government regulations, such as the Family Educational Rights and Privacy Act (FERPA), have also defined student academic freedoms. An understanding of the impact of these decisions on student freedoms needs further discussion.

The Joint Statement has not been formally adopted at the institutional level and provides no sanctions against colleges and universities that fail to abide by its provisions; as a result, its impact has been limited. Student academic freedom has not had a champion willing to place the concerns of students anywhere near the center of the academy. There have been efforts to understand the application and impact of the provisions of the Joint Statement (Cooper & Lancaster, 1995; Bryan & Mullendore, 1992) but it has not had the broad circulation across higher education that the AAUP *Statement of Principles on Academic Freedom and Tenure* continues to enjoy.

Faculty members, early in their careers, come to an understanding of the academic freedom protections afforded them, while students generally have little or no understanding of their relationship with the institution they are attending. The language of academic freedom, even the freedom to learn, is not a language with which students are familiar. If the intent of the document was to energize discussions around the topic of student academic freedom it has not been all that successful. In 2000, the AAUP approved a *Statement on Graduate Students* that includes the endorsement that "graduate students have the right to academic freedom" (p. 1), a statement that is more direct and inclusive than what is available to undergraduates.

Recognizing that the campus-as-parent was no longer viable, and in an effort to update and expand the campus-based discussions of the applicability of the Joint Statement, the National Association of Student Personnel Administrators (NASPA), a professional organization, commissioned the *Reasonable Expectations* project (Kuh, Lyons, Miller, & Trow, 1994). Kennedy (1997) details the counterpoint of academic freedom as he reminds faculty of their academic duties. *Reasonable Expectations* attempts a similar service for students, the end result of which is a series of goal statements, some of which relate directly to student freedom issues and, importantly, suggest the role colleges and universities have in providing and protecting those freedoms. The Joint Statement and its companion, *Reasonable Expectations*, are benchmarks against which progress toward student academic freedoms can be measured. These documents provide a point of departure from which serious debate on the future of student freedom could be formed. In additional, each serves as a potentially excellent, if overlooked, teaching tool to familiarize students with the concept of freedom in higher education. It is a weakness of both that they speak to the traditional higher education enterprise; having little adaptability; they will not keep pace with change and may not hold much that is useful as the higher education enterprise is redefined.

The predominate model of higher education once was the liberal arts college. It gave way to the land grant university that, in time, gave way to the multiversity, now known as the research university. The next step in the progression suggests that the university of the future may look like the University of Phoenix, maybe Western Governor's University or the British

Open University; perhaps UNext's Cardean University will be the model of our uncertain future (Duderstadt, 2000, pp. 294-295). If we do not yet know what institutions of higher education will look like, it is risky to consider what role academic freedom for students will have as the university for the 21st century unfolds. What is certain, however, is that technology will shape how knowledge is transmitted. The steady movement that marks technological advance, bringing as it does a learning-centered as opposed to the traditional teaching-centered approach, will influence the way students interact with the knowledge providers of the future.

As recently as a generation ago, and for all of the time before that, learning was a solitary task, accomplished by working alone. Now the focus is on collaboration, on working and learning together. Technology will enhance collaborative learning as virtual universities offer learning opportunities for all persons, in all areas of human knowledge, at any time, and in any place. These universities will require fewer faculty. Students will not have to come to the campus to learn, may not have to meet face to face with other learners or with professors. No longer will the campus, as a functional unit, shape student freedom. In some way, that reality should be a concern, especially for activists, because the social issues that marked the period of the 1960s are present now, albeit in somewhat different forms. If interracial marriage was an issue then, gay marriage is an issue now. Access, a concern that motivated students in the 1960s, remains an unresolved issue. As in the 1960s, today there is a war that is divisive and would be more so if the draft into military service still existed. The cost of higher education, borne more directly by the student consumer, has limited access, marking haves and have-nots based on social economic status. These and other pressing social issues are not now finding significant traction on college campuses and are unlikely to find a forum on the campuses of the future as those places will be linked more by computer terminals than by the fellowship of the campus commons. Involvement and shared values, hallmarks of the campus community, are difficult to develop in traditional settings. It remains to be seen if the internet campus will include community and, if so, the form that community will take. Without community, the student idealists of the future will be able to act only as individuals. Students will have more choices to make regarding how and what they learn but will likely have less influence over the policies that govern the process of learning. The university of the future will be market-driven, more corporate than collegial; students will be customers, sources of revenue for a corporate bottom line. Selecting from a great array of convenient and high quality offerings, students of the future will most likely exercise freedom by making choices, voting with a mouse, returning to the earliest traditions of *lernfreiheit* in Germany. Those students will have to deal with two distinct paradigms: Technology will help to maximize the abilities of students in an environment that is learner-centered, and the needs of society will demand that education be designed around the reality of lifelong learning. The risk is that, as colleges and universities move toward a future shaped by external forces, those student academic freedoms important to the learning process will be viewed as outdated and will be left behind. Structuring student freedoms in virtual environments that place emphasis on the importance of social capital will be an essential but difficult task.

As the definition of learning and the shape of the community of learners change to accommodate the Internet campus, the concepts that comprise the freedom to learn will need to be adjusted. Developing a dialogue that focuses on maintaining meaningful connections with student academic freedom as virtual learning environments evolve would go a long way toward determining the future of those freedoms. This is an important issue in need of a champion. Absent a champion, student academic freedom in higher education will be relevant only to those interested in history.

References

Argetsinger, A. (2004, October 2). Moore's GMU booking called "a mistake". *The Washington Post*, p. B5.

American Association of University Professors (AAUP). (1992). *Joint statement on rights and freedoms of students*. Washington DC: American Association of University Professors.

American Association of University Professors (AAUP). (2000). *Statement on graduate students*. Washington, DC: American Association of University Professors.

Bloustein, E. J. (1969). The new student and his role in American colleges. In W. P. Metzger, S. H. Kadish, A. DeBardeleben, & E. J. Bloustein

(Eds.), *Dimensions of academic freedom* (pp. 92-121). Urbana, IL: University of Illinois Press.

Boyer, E. (1987). *College: The undergraduate experience in America*. New York: Harper & Row.

Bryan, W. A. & Mullendore, R. H. (Eds.) (1992). *Rights, Freedoms, and Responsibilities of Students: New Directions for Student Services, No. 59*. San Francisco: Jossey-Bass.

Cohen, A. M. (1998). The shaping of American higher education. San Francisco: Jossey-Bass.

Cooper, D. L. & Lancaster, J. M. (1995). Perceived adherence to the "Joint Statement on Rights and Freedoms of Students" on college campuses. *National Association of Student Personnel Administrators Journal*, 32(Spring), 179-189. Duderstadt, J. J. (2000). *A university for the 21st century*. Ann Arbor, MI: The University of Michigan Press.

Feuer, L. S. (1969). *The conflict of generations: The character and significance of student movements*. New York: Basic Books, Inc.

Frankel, C. (1966). Rights and responsibilities in the student-college relationship. In L. Dennis & J. Kauffman, (Eds), *The college and the student* (pp. 232-251). Washington, DC: American Council on Education.

Kennedy, D. (1997). *Academic Duty*. Cambridge, MA: Harvard University Press.

Kuh, G., Lyons, J., Miller, T., & Trow, J. (1994). *Reasonable expectations: Renewing the educational compact between institutions and students*. Washington, DC: National Association of Student Personnel Administrators.

Kunen, J. (1968). *The strawberry statement-notes of a college revolutionary*. New York: Random House, Inc.

Maraniss, D. (2003). *They marched into sunlight: war and peace, Vietnam and America*. New York: Simon & Schuster.

Mayhew, L. B. (1969). *Colleges today and tomorrow*. San Francisco: Jossey-Bass.

Petrillo, L. (2004, September 22). CSU San Marcos president says Michael Moore visit would be illegal. *The San Diego Union-Tribune*, p. B3. Retrieved September 30, 2004, from http://www.signonsandiego.com

Rudolph, F. (1990). *The American college and university: A history.* Athens, GA: University of Georgia Press.

Slaughter, S. (2002). The political economy of curriculum making in American universities. In S. Brint (Ed.), *The future of the city of intellect: the changing American university* (pp. 260-289). Stanford, CA: Stanford University Press.

Student Bill of Rights. (1967). *College and University Business, 43(September),* 78-81.

Van den Haag, E. (1971). The student seizures. In S. Hook (Ed), *In defense of academic freedom* (pp. 46-60). New York: Bobbs-Merrill Company.

Williamson, E. G. & Cowan, J. L.(1966). Academic freedom for student: issues and guidelines. In L. Dennis & J. Kauffman (Eds.), *The college and the student* (pp. 252-283). Washington, DC: American Council on Education.

Chapter 2

Student Activism: A View from an Administrator

Keith M. Miser

Come gather 'round people
Wherever you roam
And admit that the waters
Around you have grown
And accept it that soon
You'll be drenched to the bone.
If your time to you
Is worth savin'
Then you better start swimmin'
Or you'll sink like a stone
For the times they are a-changin'. (Dylan, 1963)

Recollections of their first experiences with student activism in the 1960s elicit emotional responses from today's senior administrators, responses usually followed by compelling personal stories. These stories form the foundation senior administrators use to weave the fabric of the uneasy and unpredictable times of social and institutional upheaval and change. These stories also help newer generations of administrators to understand the context of the decisions of that era. These decisions—always difficult—were shaped by the response of colleges and universities to a massive cultural and historic revolution that forever changed the relationships between students with their educational institutions.

Historical Contexts

To consider and describe the administrative view of student freedom is indeed challenging. Colleges and universities are distinctive social institutions with varying values, goals, histories, and ideals. They are located in all geographical sections of the country, are public and private, large and small, and range from comprehensive, prestigious research universities to small, local community colleges. All of these distinctive features shaped their responses to student activism and to the development of new student freedoms in the 1960s. Administrators themselves vary, holding differing values, education, fears, skills, perceptions of the academy, and views of students' rights and responsibilities. Administrators also are creatures of their own pasts and their own generations' histories. These contrasts among administrators and institutional leaders shaped many administrative responses to student activism in the 1960s and contributed to the creation of policies and procedures, then and now, that significantly impact student freedom.

At the beginning of the period of dissent in the late 1960s, students were very much like their predecessors in the 1950s and early 1960s. They were career-driven and, for the most part, willing to follow the rules. They saw administrators and faculty as respected leaders and led relatively passive, uneventful lives. Colleges and universities in the early 1960s embraced a number of rules to further regulate student behavior, rules such as women's hours, drinking prohibitions, and restriction on visitation in the residence halls by members of the opposite sex. Colleges and universities also imposed a strong in loco parentis philosophy, which was the foundation for the rules and policies of that era. Little was questioned by students of the time; they followed the rules, even though the rules allowed little freedom for students. The war in Southeast Asia was almost invisible; the struggle for civil rights in America was just beginning to have national implications, and in general, constitutional rights were not viewed as extending to the regulation of student conduct in America's colleges and universities. Students who did have concerns about rules on campus were pushed aside by administrative staff and scolded for complaining about something that could not be changed. This scene was about to change with the arrival of the late 1960s.

The war in Vietnam became part of everyday life as almost every American faced the prospect of a family member being drafted to serve the country in this struggle. Many of the young men and women who became part of the armed forces were wounded or killed, a trauma repeated daily on the television news. Vietnam was the first war to be recorded and broadcast daily in such a manner. It was a difficult war for college students to understand, and a traumatic time for the friends and families of those who died, young people who just a few months earlier had been part of their lives (Miller, 1987). Issues of life and death in Vietnam, civil rights struggles, deaths, and bombings became part of the lives of thousands of students on campuses across America.

In addition to the civil rights struggles and protests against the war in Vietnam, local rules and regulations at colleges and universities began to be challenged. This challenge of rules was particularly true when individuals who had served in Vietnam came back to campus to find they were subjected to restrictive social rules, punitive discipline systems, and irrelevant curriculum. These issues—civil rights, social rules, curriculum content, and the war—joined to cause students to express anger, disillusionment, and disgust. Eventually students took to the streets in protest. The individual student dissenters then merged into a tide of individuals demanding change, angry people who expected administrators to respond quickly and completely to their demands. Groups of dissenting students roamed campuses and surrounding neighborhoods to demand freedom, equality, social justice, and constitutional guarantees that they believed strongly should be extended to all campus activities, ranging from freedom of the campus newspaper to rules regulating student residential living to curriculum reform. The turmoil of this era became the foundation for a basic cultural shift among America's youth. Many of the values, concerns, and anger of youth at this time were reinforced and advanced by the contemporary music of the era and the visual and performing arts of the day. Music and anger became the vehicles which propelled much of the cultural change on college and university campuses, resulting in a long-lasting youth revolution.

Campus activism caused institutions to react but often the intemperate actions of the campus leaders served to refocus the protesters, making the institution itself the target and student rights the issue.

College and university leaders of the late '60s were unprepared for the cultural change and dissent they found themselves confronting. Some senior administrators of that era resigned under fire or in protest, or retired early. Some saw the student-led revolution as evil and communist-inspired and feared that it would lead to the destruction of America or, at least, to the demise of the spirit of campus life they had known and were protecting.

Colleges resisted the student movement and began using legal processes and state police power to challenge and, in some cases, harass the students. The beleaguered administrators making these decisions were products of their own generation, which generally believed in the rightness of America. Some had an authoritarian management style adopted from the military, in which many of the senior administrators of that era had served. They believed sincerely that they should resist, challenge, and defeat the sweeping demands for change they were witnessing. Viewed from their perspective, they had good and well-developed intentions for resisting change. They had developed the policies and practices they were defending, and those polices and practices had served the institution well, allowing the university to develop into a quality institution. Because they resisted change, these senior administrators were often singled out by students. Also, administrators resistant to change were frequently criticized by faculty members, and in general, the actions, philosophy, and direction of many of these administrators created or contributed to a chasm between students and their institutions.

Another group of administrators believed that the demands being expressed by the dissenting students were appropriate and that colleges and universities needed to change. This group, although supporting the content of the demands for change, often opposed the tactics used by students to advance their concerns. Classroom disruption, building takeovers and violence were abhorred by this group of administrators. They respected students as idealists and tried to use current laws and policies to work with the dissenters. Supportive of the advances being sought by civil rights groups, recognizing the need to change hypocritical campus student life policies, and, in general, opposed to the position of the United States in Southeast Asia, these administrators and faculty attempted to find common ground. This group, however, was trapped between angry, rebellious students their desire to support students on principle. They saw the newly emerging student freedoms as positive and as a welcome change, but were unsupportive of strategies that seemed to destroy rather than recreate. Most of all, they rejected violence and disruption as tactics to be used by students on college campuses.

Yet a third group of administrators agreed with student demands even more strongly as not only positive, but also necessary. This view of change was positive, and these administrators saw themselves as university agents of change—the links between the students and colleges and universities that resisted change. On many campuses, this group of often young and, almost always, progressive administrators helped with communication, defining principles, and working effectively with students through the process of dissent and institutional change.

By the mid-1970s, with the war at an end, the campuses returned to a calm and more peaceful condition. Colleges and universities, however, had been changed forever.

Students had gained sweeping new freedoms and, importantly, constitutional support for them. The concept of in loco parentis was diminished if not destroyed, although some administrators, parents, and alumni continued with the expectation that it would still be the practice in higher education. Students at the end of this era were more in charge of their own lives than any previous generation of students. Student protests had created new freedoms which resulted in a new era for American higher education.

After the many battles, discussions, and confrontations, everything in higher education seemed changed. The students' freedom of speech and assembly were guaranteed and widely respected on most campuses. Colleges and universities rewrote judicial policies and discipline codes to assure due process and fairness. Public institutions could not discriminate against students in organizations or through admissions polices and procedures, housing accommodations, or in any other way. The institutions changed student residential living rules and addressed women's hours.

These changes, now that the upheaval of dissent had passed, were accepted by most administrators. Also, by the mid-1980s, colleges and universities began hiring junior administrators and faculty members who were themselves dissenters in the '60s. This change in generations of administrators resulted in progressive changes in administrative approaches, personal values, communication styles, and the care for students. Many of this new generation of administrators and faculty strongly supported the new freedoms and often were seen as socially liberal in their approach to administration. As was the case of their predecessors, they were a reflection of their own era.

Interestingly, in the 1980s and 1990s students were increasingly socially conservative. Administrators of that era, however, were the product of the 1960s and '70s and often were more socially and politically liberal than the students. This situation—the result of the change in generations of administrators—was the very opposite of the 1960s, when students were seen as liberal and administrators as conservative. In the 1990s, conflicts sometimes arose between administrative personnel and students because students were willing to relinquish some freedom for things, like facilities and campus security, while administrative leaders argued that student freedom should be preserved at all costs.

As the millennium approached, a new generation of students began to emerge that was clearly more active on social issues, more concerned about others, and more interested in improving the human condition. Students of that era defined their concerns in terms of environmental priorities, animal rights, globalization, and working conditions in "sweatshops." They demanded that colleges and universities refrain from investing in companies doing business in South Africa, some Pacific Islands and Southeast Asian nations, and, in general, any nation or region that did not support human rights in the workplace.

Advances in technology armed students with cell phones, the Internet, text messaging, wi-fi, and other forms of improved communications that, in many ways, have become the effective and efficient instruments of dissent today. Students have mobilized in recent years, as agents of change addressing contemporary issues such as the war in Iraq (Hostetler, 2003). Students and other members of campus communities have demanded freedom for the Iraqis from the oppression of the United States, which many saw as just as bad, or worse, than the oppression of the Saddam Hussein regime. As Mast & Mast (1996) stated so well, "Most of the movement of the '60s failed to understand and refused to accept that the real mass mobilizing potential lay in the age-old material interest of the people" (p. 432).

Changing Perspectives

How did dissent and the thirst for freedom of the 1960s and '70s change the administrative perspective? In reviewing administrative responses and approaches to student freedom and activism, several themes emerge. Probably the most dramatic shift was the demise of the in loco parentis doctrine as the foundation for defining the relationship between students and their institutions. Typical conditions of the 1960s— strict enforcement of too many rules and policies aimed at controlling students in every aspect of college life— were challenged and ultimately defeated. These policies and activities were put in place to reinforce positive behavior on the part of students and were logical outcomes of the traditional and long-standing belief that the institution acted in place of parents. Colleges and universities accepted this role, and parents, for the most part, expected it. Drinking was not allowed on campus, and there were many dress codes: coats and ties were required of men, and dresses were required of women in the dining halls and at many facilities on campuses. Student newspapers were reviewed and often censored by campus administrators. Due process was frequently not part of the judicial system, and sanctions were used on some campuses to rid the community of trouble makers, undesirables, and those who openly questioned the authority of officials.

Student affairs administrators spent a great percentage of their time enforcing institutional behavioral rules in the early 1960s. Student activists demanded equal treatment for men and women, freedom of the press for student publications, judicial and discipline systems that observed due process rights, and universities that recognized students as adults. They demanded an end to the long-standing tradition of the institution acting as parent. As a result of the demands of student activists, lawsuits were brought against colleges and universities challenging the in loco parentis concept. Enforcement of overly strict, often meaningless, rules resulted in punitive action against students, fueling protests and increasing support for the rights of students (Miser, 1988). Student activists often were successful in their legal challenges against student codes of conduct, and, by the time the 1980s arrived, student life rules, policies, and procedures bore little resemblance to similar policies of the 1960s. As many educators and lawyers described it, the constitution had finally arrived on the campus. Wynkoop (2002), describing the changes at Indiana University, stated, "Discussing students today, they have no concept of women's hours or dress codes. Women and men have more freedom to live where they want, with whom they want, and how they want today than they did before the 1960s" (p. 185).

Some administrators saw this movement away from in loco parentis as the destruction of higher education. They retired, resigned, or sought positions outside of education. Others in administrative leadership roles welcomed the change and led the efforts to transform the relationship between the universities and students to one that respected students as adults. Although these sweeping changes caused some loss of formal institutional authority, most administrators saw the change as positive, especially after several relatively trouble-free years during the transition. Administrators began to aggressively develop programs, initiatives, and activities designed to help assure the academic and personal success of students. Student affairs programs and activities shifted their emphasis from in loco parentis and rule enforcement to student development and programming that would assist and enhance the personal and intellectual growth of students. Discipline systems were revised to assure due process and campus policies were modified to adhere to changing federal, state, and local law regarding the rights and freedoms of students. Students accepted these new freedoms with enthusiasm. As change occurred, many administrators believed that if the new freedoms were granted, universities would lose the responsibility for teaching moral and ethical behavior, respect, and responsibility. In rare instances, some institutional administrators and faculty leaders predicted a complete breakdown of the social order on campus and the eventual demise of the American system of higher education. Students, for the most part, did not abuse their new-found freedom and acted responsibly as adult leaders in their campus communities. This response of students contributed greatly to the relatively rapid acceptance of the freedoms by campus leaders. As a result, student personnel staff, because of the working relationships they formed with students, could make claim to being educators, contributors to the student learning process, and not just disciplinarians.

Another important change that came from the shift in the legal relationship between students and the university was that of change and growth in professional organizations such as the NASPA, the American Personnel and Guidance Association (APGA), and the National Association of Women

Deans and Counselors (NAWDAC). These student personnel professional organizations had for many years built training and professional development programs to assist deans of men and women in their enforcement roles. Suddenly, with the arrival of new student freedoms, those organizations faced rapid change, focusing instead on student academic and personal development.

A second significant change, from an administrative perspective, was the arrival of a national financial aid movement and system that, in many ways, created and cultivated freedom on each college and university campus. The Higher Education Act of 1965 created the foundation for a national effort to increase student access to institutions of postsecondary education. Before this dramatic national change, most colleges and universities served middle- and upper-class students. Administrators, especially in student affairs administration, welcomed this change and created new financial aid processes and opportunities to assure that all eligible students could participate. The growth in the availability of financial aid for college and university students was, in many ways, another opportunity to assure freedom for students, especially low-income students. Financial aid allowed them some relief from the requirement to work an unreasonable number of hours per week just to pay their student bills. The Higher Education Act of 1965 allowed all students to participate fully in educational activities, become student leaders, and be fully involved and engaged in cocurricular activities, not just the more privileged financially. This sweeping change of national financial aid for masses of students created economic freedom for thousands of students across America.

Another dramatic change from an administrative perspective was the engagement of campuses in the broader American civil rights movement. Although student activism began on many campuses over local student life issues and the war in Vietnam, many campuses also saw activism in the form of demands for increased access for ethnically and culturally diverse students. In the southern states, many colleges and universities prior to the 1960s did not permit the enrollment of African Americans. In the North, institutions may have been more supportive of diversity, but many practiced a subtle, controlling form of discrimination. National student organizations such as the Student Nonviolent Coordinating Committee (SNCC) mobilized students from both the North and the South, both majority and minority students, to demand equal treatment of underrepresented students and to demand that students and campuses be free from discrimination. Marches, sit-ins, and demonstrations occurred on many campuses on issues relating to the civil rights challenges of this era. Often the dissent was targeted at local communities, local law enforcement issues, and local merchants who practiced discrimination in their businesses.

In response to local dissent, national movements, legal challenges, and the support of hundreds of students, faculty, and administrative staff, institutions of postsecondary education finally began to move away from discriminatory and exclusionary practices. Two decades later, nearly all public universities had ended overt discriminatory admissions practices. On many campuses, this fragile and difficult change was led by key administrators in response not only to student dissent but to their own values and beliefs. These administrative leaders often stood alone and were often attacked by local citizens, elected officials, and faculty. They were many times labeled as subversive or communists for their support of change in this difficult era. In the end, campuses with the strongest administrative leadership became communities that, at least in principle and ideal, were free from discrimination and were supportive of students representing diverse races, cultures, and ethnicities.

Today, a mere 30 years later, it is difficult to believe that these overt, destructive, and pervasive discriminatory practices actually were supported at so many institutions for such a long time. Most administrators looking back see this as a very positive era of change and are proud to be part of the movements of that era that helped shape the philosophy of diversity that is now prevalent on our nation's college and university campuses.

Lessons Learned

What were the lessons learned from the era of dissent, protest, and institutional transformation? How will these lessons serve higher education as each college and university faces the future? One lesson is that significant institutional transformation can happen; strong administrative and faculty support can help create change through leadership, result in coalition building, and provide moral and legal direction for both students and campuses in a time of social upheaval. The strong administrative leaders who took bold, imaginative steps to do what they believed ethically and educationally correct for their communities are seen today as vitally important to the changes that occurred. Many of those leaders took steps to remove symbols, policies and practices that reinforced racism before protests even occurred. They changed policies without being presented a list of demands. They supported dissent and welcomed new student freedoms, and yet respected the rights of those who spoke against their decisions while others battled in vain to protect their antiquated system of control over student conduct. The leaders who resisted change were not successful and did not change as persons or as administrators while the world around them was changing. Strong, value-based leadership clearly was the most successful administrative approach to enhance, reinforce, and lead institutional transformation.

Another critical lesson is how to view student activism and dissent. In the early period of the 1960s, dissent was almost universally viewed by administrators as negative, illegal, disruptive, threatening, and intolerable. Dissent that occurred on college and university campuses, even within the bounds of university policy and within students' first amendment rights, often was seen as inappropriate or illegal. Some administrators of that era fought dissent and change using every mechanism at their command. For the most part, these college and university administrators failed their students and their institutions by not adapting to the change. Today, administrative leaders should and often do accept dissent as an important part of a vibrant and constructive campus community. Present-day dissent often involves students in social-change paradigms, such as the Peace Corps, Teach for America, Service-Learning options, alternative Spring Breaks, and other specially designed campus-based programs to encourage commitment and involvement. Progressive administrators today encourage students to take stands on social issues and to educate themselves about the methods and options leading to social change. The 2001 Wingspread Conference (Long, 2001), was convened to reshape the national direction on student civic engagement. Brown (2003) outlined the significance of the Wingspread Conference and its recommendations as a blueprint for civic engagement for college students for the next decade and a vehicle to advance new freedoms through social change. Today, student involvement in social action issues is seen as positive, tied to the learning process, and something to be encouraged, all for the purpose of producing leaders who will be effective in their families, communities, and schools long after graduation.

Another important lesson to be learned is that there are cycles to student activism and dissent. There are periods when students reach out as a group to others, issuing a class demand for change. Research conducted by Levine and Cureton (1998) shows cycles of behavior common among college students over almost one hundred years. One cycle is defined as individual ascendancy. During these years students are less activist, more politically conservative, more isolated, and less interested in international concerns; memberships in fraternities and sororities rise and religious participation increases. The opposite cycle is that of community ascendancy where trends in behavior move in the opposite direction. The activism and dissent of the late 1960s follows the cycle of community ascendancy. Currently, many believe that the country is moving into a new period of community ascendancy, which could be the precursor to another period of student activism (Levine & Cureton, 1998). If so, college administrators will be tested on the lessons of the '60s. The challenge for higher education, particularly for student personnel administrators, is to be prepared for that test.

Another lesson is that student engagement in activism tends to promote learning. Researchers have found that retention, student learning, and student development can be enhanced by student involvement in the learning process (Kuh, Schuh, & Whitt, 1991). Dissent and service learning are vehicles by which students become involved in learning both inside and outside the classroom. Recently, the National Survey of Student Engagement has been used to assess student learning entirely from a student perspective. Service learning and dissent are both ways to be involved to create change while learning.

Finally, higher education administrators have learned that the relatively recent use of technology will drive student dissent and student struggles for freedom in the future. In the 1960s, calls for rallies, marches, and dissent activities were usually broadcast by posters, mailings, telephone calls, and the skilled but limited use of local media. Today, with the popular use of the Internet, cell phones, and text messaging, thousands of potential dissenting students can be mobilized by a relatively few number of organizers, a point detailed elsewhere in this book. The organizers can be located anywhere in the world. Rheingold (2003) calls these groups of individuals "smart mobs" (p. i), and he believes that they have tremendous power and will influence public policy throughout the world in the future. For example, the coordinator of Moveon.org, Eli Pariser, age 22, can organize a protest of 750,000 followers using only e-mail and text messaging (Taylor, 2003).

Many of today's students use the Internet as a vehicle for dissent. By flooding the email boxes of college presidents, Senators, or the President of the United States, individuals can and do have an effective electronic voice that can be heard and can influence decisions. This technology in some format will certainly be the organizing foundation for communication in future campus dissent.

Summary

Campus dissent, student activism, and efforts for student freedom are woven into the rich fabric of postsecondary education today. Since the early days at Harvard Yard and Yale, University, students have spoken out on issues that are critical to them and common to society. American higher education is stronger today and the learning environment is more vital because students in past decades have challenged administrators, faculty, and members of the campus community to consider alternative paradigms and new ways of thinking. As these students gained new freedoms through persistent dissent, they helped to redefine the social institutions of America. The ideal of student freedom—freedom to learn, to associate, and to speak—is our basic American freedom. The struggles that students articulate today are the struggles of all members of our campus community and of American society. The advent of the new student freedoms in many ways has made the work of student affairs administrators more closely aligned with the educational mission of a university. For most administrators, being a teacher is much more complex and challenging than being an enforcer. For most administrators, today's approach is much more professionally challenging and personally fulfilling.

References

Brown, P. M. (2003, October). *Student activism: Making the world work better.* Presentation at Student Affairs Development Seminar, University of Hawai'i at Hilo.

Dylan, R. (1963). *The Times They Are A-Changin'.* Retrieved January 16, 2005, from http://www.bobdylan.com/songs/times.html

Hostetler, M. J. (2003). College student activism: Then and now. *In Touch with Student Services, 11*(2), 9.

Kuh, G., Schuh, J. & Whitt, E.(1991). *Involving colleges: Successful approaches to fostering student learning and development outside the classroom.* San Francisco: Jossey-Bass.

Levin, A. & Cureton, J. (1998). *When hope and fear collide: A portrait of today's college student.* San Francisco: Jossey-Bass.

Long, S. (2001). *The new student politics: The Wingspread statement on student civic engagement.* Providence, R.I.: Campus Compact, Brown University.

Mast, R. H.. & Mast, A. B. (1996). *Autobiography of protest in Hawai'i.* Honolulu: University of Hawai'i Press.

Miller, J. (1987). *Democracy is in the streets.* New York: Simon and Schuster.

Miser, K. M. (1988). *Student affairs and campus dissent: Reflection of the past and challenge for the future.* Washington, DC: National Association of Student Personnel Administrators.

Rheingold, H. (2003). *Smart mobs: The next social revolution.* Cambridge, MA: Perseus.

Taylor, C. (2003, March 10). Technology: Day of the smart mobs. *Time, 161,* 53.

Wynkoop, M. A. (2002). *Dissent in the heartland: The sixties at Indiana University.* Bloomington, IN: Indiana University Press.

Chapter 3

Campus Subcultures and the Emergence of Student Freedom in American Higher Education

Louis C. Vaccaro

Any consideration of student freedom and activism in American higher education must account for the influence of the subcultures that exist among the students exercising that freedom. "Student subcultures, as they are called today, existed long before the 1960s, when many colleges and universities in the United States erupted in a series of rebellious outbursts aimed in part at those in positions of campus authority. It does not imply any particular set of beliefs or activities. Rather, student subcultures encompass all the myriad ways in which college students define themselves, view their professors and fellow students, create various groups and associations, and explore ways of making sense of, and perhaps influencing, collegiate and individual behavior.

Indeed, those who have studied the history and development of American higher education know only too well that student subcultures have existed almost as long as American colleges and universities themselves, even at the earliest universities in medieval times. In a word, the phenomenon of student subcultures is generational, defined as:

> ...a whole body of conceptions and images of problems and situations and of proper and justifiable solutions of them arrived at by the students; in part passed along from one generation of students to another, in part apparently rediscovered—or at least reinforced—by each succeeding generation as they pass through the same experiences. (Hughes, Becker, & Geer, 1962, p. 518)

Within any particular institution there usually exists a dominant student subculture: a general set of beliefs, values, and attitudes shared by most or all of the students. The dominant student culture may mirror or refute the core ideals and values of the institution as a whole, but in either event can exert a powerful influence on an institution's culture and administration. Those in positions of campus power and authority know through experience that any effort to change institutional policies and/or practices must take into account the values of the prevailing student subculture and must attempt to obtain the students' support for any proposed change.

A historical review of undergraduate collegiate life in the United States (Vaccaro and Covert, 1969, p. 35) recognizes three dominant student subcultures, two of which emerged in the late 18th century. The first of these is called *college life* or *the culture of the college man* (Horowitz, 1987, p. 16), typically identified with sports, clubs, and fraternities accompanied by ample parties. The second student subculture is known as the *outsiders* (Horowitz, 1987, p. 16). This term refers to those students who shun the culture of the college man and everything that term stands for: hedonism, campus sports, college as fun. For the outsiders, college is a time to prepare for the future. The original 18th century outsiders typically were preparing for the ministry; later outsiders were preparing to enter more secular professions. Even later, especially following WWII, American colleges and universities welcomed hundreds of thousands of adult students, veterans, and commuters—all new outsiders. These later outsiders, like their 18th century counterparts, regarded the faculty as their allies, something the members of the college life subculture typically did not.

The third subculture, the *rebels*, emerged in the early 20th century, also in opposition to the prevailing college life subculture. According to Horowitz (1987), "College rebels fought the social distinctions that sorted out college students and reveled in the difference, not uniformity" (p. 16). The rebels subculture generally consisted of students whose backgrounds, ethnicity and religious affiliations kept them out of college life, although their interests combined the academic orientation of the outsiders with the hedonism of the college man (Horowitz, 1987, p. 18).

The formations of the various student subcultures represent, in a way, different group responses to the challenges faced by most, if not all, students at the same institution at the same time. Knowingly or unknowingly, students tend to group together to succeed academically while learning how to make friends and to affect organizations and other people. While some student subcultures are loosely organized, casually joined, and often informal, some have elaborate ceremonies and rituals for incoming members (e.g., initiation of pledges in sororities and fraternities, orientation of freshmen) as well as various mechanisms of social control (e.g., grade-point requirements for membership, dress codes). Somewhat steadily though, beginning in the 18th century and continuing through the 1950s, more and more students exhibited individualism and the desire for more academic, social, and political freedom. As might have been expected, college authorities used various means to control and/or thwart the undergraduates' push for individual freedom, sometimes contributing further to the students' desire for freedom from institutional controls.

As Horowitz (1987) states:

> [C]ultural rebels, less easy to describe because their struggles were more inward and more diverse, withheld their assent throughout the 1940s and 1950s. Nonconformity began to take a common shape on campus in the late 1950s as alienated youth responded to new artistic currents and to the promise of psychic release from conformist America. Less visibly independent-minded undergraduates quietly pursued their own ends. (p. 172)

And woven throughout these ends were the students' intense desire for more freedom—personal, social, and political. At the same time, consciously or not, students were objecting to and rebelling at the rules and restrictions placed on them by their parents, churches, college authorities, and others in positions of authority.

One group, however, was more than conscious of its quest for more freedom. This group was composed primarily of the veterans of WWII and the Korean conflict. Following their wartime service, they arrived on campus in droves for the vocational and academic rewards that college offered, completely uninterested in college life. These students were older, often married, experienced, and most importantly, constituted a majority of the student body, but they were not generally appreciated by their younger classmates. As one traditional-age undergraduate put it, "All they care about is their schoolwork. They're grinds, every one of them. It's books, books all the time" (Efron, 1949, p. 21).

Post-WWII enrollments surged from 1946 through the 1960s, as veterans of both WWII and the Korean conflict swarmed to colleges and universities, causing a boom in campus construction and expansion. At the same time, college and university administrators scrambled to keep abreast of the growth in enrollments and the needs of both traditional and nontraditional student populations. Some administrators, in their quest to maintain order and stability within their institutions, failed to differentiate between the needs of traditional and nontraditional students. One example of this phenomenon was the administrations' efforts to maintain and defend the centuries-old policy of *in loco parentis*. While well-intended and obviously welcomed by the parents of traditional-age students, the policy was viewed more negatively by the more mature, worldly, and less agreeable nontraditional students. It was this attitude displayed by the more mature nontraditional students that prompted some of the more daring members of the rebel subculture to question not only the policy of in loco parentis but also other traditional university policies and practices which stood in their way of obtaining more social and intellectual freedom.

The veterans and the other older, more mature students brought the consciousness of the outsiders to the fore of campus culture. They came to college seriously, totally uninterested in college life, and soon found themselves growing impatient with the imprecision of professors who had seldom before been challenged by students. Many of the veterans and returning older students, like the rebels, desired a clearer vocational direction to their course of studies.

The college men complained that the veterans and other older students were wrecking their experience by raising the grading curve and failing to participate in extracurricular activities. Moreover, claimed the traditional college men, the veterans balked at established and revered college traditions. At Lehigh University in Pennsylvania, for example, the veterans refused to wear the brown cap required of freshmen or light the cigarettes of upper classmen (Horowitz, 1987). Clearly, the influence of veterans and the other returning older students had a strong influence on the shaping of the campus culture of the 1950s and '60s. Though they remained on campus for only a few years, they left institutions very different from the ones they found, partly by strengthening or invigorating the rebel subculture. By the late

1950s, observers of American higher education perceived a divided rather than unified campus environment. During this time, the impact of these changes plus the changes taking place in society and the American economy and its relation to higher education was clear. Burton Clark and Martin Trow (1961), described major changes within the changing campus culture at the time:

> Clark saw the college population divided into several different subcultures: collegiate, bohemian, vocational, and academic. Once organizations hiring graduates and professional schools became seriously concerned with transcripts, students were less likely to join the collegiate subculture and more likely to identify with the vocational or academic. The number of students who can afford to ignore the record is diminishing. As a result of this and other tendencies, the collegiate subculture, whose panoply of big-time sports and fraternity weekends has provided the dominant image of college life since the end of the 19th century, is now in decline
>
> Clark's typology met severe criticism, especially among those uncomfortable with the use of the concept of subculture for student groups. He and his critics were both right and wrong. College men and women and rebels (the students whom Clark calls "collegiate" and "bohemian") have formed distinct subcultures; the outsiders (Clark's "academic" and "vocational") have not, but have remained within their cultures of origin. (Horowitz, 1987, p. 190)

Clark and Trow's study had the misfortune of being published before the heat and turmoil of the 1960s really developed, a time when educators and the general public paid little attention to students who labored to make good grades and who were positioning themselves to take advantage of opportunities inherent in the new technocratic order. Later, as the growing undergraduate radicalism seized center stage, public interest and the media focused on student discontent and campus protest (Vaccaro & Covert, 1969).

Whatever the specific causes, no one surveying the campus scene in 1959 could have predicted the cataclysmic changes that erupted in the 1960s. In

May 1969, from the vantage point of Harvard, Berkeley, or Columbia, the established campus social order appeared to be disintegrating. At more than 350 colleges and universities, students were on strike (Vaccaro & Covert, 1969, p. 85)). Some observers estimated that more than one half of the campuses nationwide experienced some kind of demonstration (Vaccaro & Covert, 1969, pp. 86-87). Students seized campus buildings, radicals took university administrators hostage, and campus security police were embattled. Fueled by the growing discontent with America's involvement in Vietnam and its perceived failing foreign policy, sizeable segments of the undergraduate community joined forces to create a mass revolutionary campus atmosphere aimed at influencing if not toppling, those in positions of power and authority, both inside and outside the university administration. Students at hundreds of colleges and universities refused to attend classes; they staged demonstrations aimed at crippling "the system" and bringing down the administrations at several of America's universities. The campus rebellions spread, attracting a broad segment of America's middle-class youth as well as the more antiestablishment radicals. Clearly, the clarion call for more freedom struck a sympathetic note across the nation's campuses. And while the spark may have been the initial antiwar, antigovernment feelings of thousands of campus radicals, the fuel that kept the movement going included the pent up feelings of disdain held by many undergraduates toward their college and university administrators, and their outmoded policies of treating undergraduate students as children rather than as maturing adults.

As the movement gained momentum and university administrations gave in to the incessant demands of the students, greater freedoms were granted in the areas of academic, social, political, and college-wide policies. One result of the increased freedoms granted, often grudgingly, was a gradual merging of the campus subcultures. Distinctions between the collegiates, the outsiders, and the rebels became blurred, and what became important for most students was the new sense of freedom that pervaded America's campuses. There emerged a sense among undergraduate students that their efforts, their somewhat united movement, had paved the way for increased campus freedoms and was due, at least in part, to their collaboration or cooperation.

Sporadic efforts were made to reestablish pre-1960s order and traditions, but it was not to be. As Horowitz states:

> The campus of the past did not return in the same form, however. The 1960s had reshaped the college world. Fraternities and sororities lost their appeal. For the first time in their history, they declined both in membership and in prestige. Many houses at the lower end of the pecking order closed. Schools suspended college rituals, due to lack of interest. Student government seemed passé. The hegemony of college men and women and the prestige of their activities ended. Divisions still existed between students, but no longer operated to sort them out hierarchically. The structural consequences of the 1960s remained on campus after students had turned from protest to serious study. (Horowitz, 1987, p. 244)

Not only at America's flagship universities, but also at hundreds of lesser known colleges and universities nationwide, undergraduate students began to enjoy freedoms that had been dreams only a few years before. There was a feeling among undergraduate students that they were still not being taken seriously but that their protests—sometimes peaceful, sometimes not—had paved the way for the freedoms that today are taken for granted on America's college and university campuses. Gone were the days of restrictive campus policies pertaining to individual and social behaviors. More liberal policies governing academic and campus political life became the order of the day. A new sense of academic and political seriousness began to pervade American higher education, largely as the result of undergraduate students' efforts to shape and reform their campuses.

Although current student attitudes and behaviors are difficult to measure, there is increasing evidence that today's students are less prone to join or belong to student groups, clubs, and movements (Levine & Cureton, 1998). Contemporary students are much more inclined to form their own individual opinions and judgments based on their assessment of current ideas, ideologies, and trends and are less likely to be swayed by the opinions of others, including faculty and administrators (Levine & Cureton, 1998). Thus, today's dominant student subculture can more accurately be labeled as nonconforming. Given the tumultuous '60s and '70s, it is understandable that today's students are less likely to be attracted to or to be motivated to participate in mass movements; they are more likely be detached, observers rather than participants, and to form their own opinions based on their assessment of current needs and issues. When students are attracted to issues, research (Levine & Cureton, 1998) suggests that multiculturalism and the cost of college continue to receive the most attention. Multiculturalism remains a concern on campuses and it is likely that identifiable student subcultures will form around both ethnic groups and the cause of multiculturalism.

Indeed, one can also conclude that whatever good resulted from the years of campus revolt and upheaval, today's students are much more inclined to find and follow their own individual way based on their own serious reflective thoughts than they are to commit themselves to a restrictive organization or subculture within the university community. Students today are thus less connected with the university and their fellow students due to technology, employment, and other outside responsibilities. Institutions have had to change dramatically as well in the last 35 years. While the college men, rebels, and outsiders are still identifiable on most campuses, the most rapid growth of late seems to be in the group of those to belong to none of the three. Although generally disconnected from traditional campus life, these students surely share some common interests and concerns, some of which are likely to conflict with those of more traditional students, such as scheduling of evening and weekend classes. It is not difficult to imagine, then, that these students will somehow coalesce into a new subculture (see Redhead, 1993).

Those who lived through the campus turmoil of the 1960s are better able to grasp and appreciate the cataclysmic changes that have reshaped America's colleges and universities during the past four decades. To be sure, contemporary campus life continues to evolve and redefine itself. But one thing is clear: the various student subcultures dating back to the earliest times have helped reshape contemporary campus cultures and mores and eventually the state of student freedom in American higher education. What is not so clear is whether the modern transformation of higher education will result in the development of a new student subculture, and what impact that might have on the future of higher education (Whitt, 1993). In the past, student subcultures shaped the campus; one wonders if in the future it will be the campus that shapes the subcultures.

Finding answers to the question of how student subcultures will affect the academy in the future is difficult at best. What is not so clear is where all this is going. There has been an ebb and flow between student cultures: the college man in the '50s, the rebels in the '60s, and the outsiders in the '70s. For a while in the '80s, the college man subculture made a come-back but, while still around, it is no longer dominant. The rebels, who in the '60s were so strong as to have changed the campuses and higher education, exist but are largely silent and invisible. What may happen to so elusive a phenomenon is impossible to discern. However, one thing is certain— whatever the shape and nature of future student subcultures, they will influence nearly every aspect of American higher education including the curriculum, the extracurriculum and, to a lesser degree, the way our colleges and universities are governed and organized (Slobin, 1993; Ben-Yehuda, 1990). To expect otherwise is to ignore the past. The lesson from the unrest of the 1960s is that student subcultures changed society; so the real question is: What impact will the yet-to-emerge student subcultures have on the larger society? How will these changes affect American society? If the past is any indication of future trends, we can expect more than a modicum of influence and social change.

References

Ben-Yehuda, N. (1990) *The politics of morality and deviance.* Albany, NY: SUNY Press.

Clark, B. R. & Trow, M. (1961). The organizational context. In T. Newcomb & K. Wilson (Eds.), *College peer groups: Problems and prospects for research* (pp. 17-71). Chicago: Aldine Publishing Co.

Efron, E. (1949, June 16). The two Joes meet—Joe College, Joe Veteran, *The New York Times Magazine,* 21.

Horowitz, H. L. (1987). *Campus life: Undergraduate cultures from the end of the eighteenth century to the present.* Chicago: University of Chicago Press.

Hughes, E. C., Becker, H. S., & Geer, B. (1962). Student culture and academic effort. In N. Sanford (Ed.), *The American college*. New York: John Wiley and Sons.

Levine, A. & Cureton, J. S. (1998). *When hope and fear collide: A portrait of today's college student*. San Francisco: Jossey-Bass.

Newcomb, T. M. & Wilson, E. K. (Eds.). (1961). College peer groups: Problems and prospects for research. Chicago: Aldine Publishing Company.

Redhead, S. (Ed.). (1993). *Rave off!: Politics and deviance in contemporary youth culture*. Brookfield, Aldershot, Hampshire England: Ashgate Publishing.

Slobin, M. (1993). *Subcultural sounds: Micromusics of the west*. Hanover, NH: Wesleyan University Press.

Vaccaro, L. C. & Covert, J. T. (Eds.). (1969). *Student freedom in American higher education*. Columbia, NY: Teachers College Press.

Whitt, E. J. (1993). Making the familiar strange: Discovering culture. In G.D. Kuth (Ed.), *Cultural perspectives in student affairs work*. Washington, DC: American College Personnel Association.

Chapter 4

Diversity and Student Freedom

Corlisse D. Thomas and André McKenzie

No present-day discussion of student freedom on college campuses would be complete without a consideration of its relationship to diversity. By definition, the terms *diverse* and *multicultural* are broad in scope on today's campuses and encompass a broad spectrum of students. As colleges and universities strive to extend opportunities to all segments of the population and adjust their institutional objectives to be responsive to various student groups, an expanding number of students can be included within the terms diverse and multicultural. Diversity on college campuses once referred only to students of color, namely Black, Asian, Latino, and Native Americans. The expanding definition of diversity now includes broader and more subtle differences in race, ethnicity, national origin, gender, age, sexual orientation, class, ability, and religion. This chapter addresses the emergence of students of color on college campuses, the accompanying campus responses to their growth, and the current questions that campuses must face in order to accommodate and promote diversity. Additionally, we will consider how the expanded definition of diversity has changed the understanding of students and provided new perspectives on student freedoms.

The Emergence of Students of Color on Campus

The history of students of color on American college campuses predates the political and social upheaval of the 1960s. Although the numbers were small, there are records of college attendance by nonwhite students as early as the 1600s (Kidwell, 1994; Wright, 1989). The genesis of educational institutions specifically for nonwhite groups began with Indian Colleges in the 1600s. Wright (1989) points out that "Indians in fact offered the impetus for establishing and maintaining among the nation's most enduring and prestigious halls of higher learning—such elite institutions as Harvard College, the College of William and Mary, and Dartmouth College" (p.53). The Morrill Act of 1890 established specific colleges for Blacks following the end of the Civil War. Although a few such colleges existed in northern states, this legislative mandate resulted in a proliferation of colleges for Blacks in the south. Both Indian and Black colleges had significant difficulty at their inception. The establishment of these schools was viewed by some as a means of civilizing or acculturating these populations and by others as the way to keep them separate from Whites enrolled in college. The result was a variety of institutions, some culturally repressive, many inferior to White colleges, but others that offered social acceptance and support that were not available to these students at other schools.

The 1960s saw a change in enrollment trends for students of color. Black students began attending predominantly White institutions in larger numbers, thereby changing the role of Black colleges but not entirely ending their growth. Tribal colleges for Native Americans were established late in the decade, and specific colleges and universities were designated as Hispanic Serving Institutions (HSI). The creation of colleges and universities to serve students of color filled a critical need and offered them access to higher education as these populations have emerged from various forms of oppression. The challenge of integrating students of color into the bigger picture of American higher education soon took center stage. As they began attending predominantly White institutions, these students routinely faced hostility, ignorance, violence, rejection, neglect, and overt discrimination.

The enactment of laws such as the Civil Rights Act was the primary factor leading to the increase in multicultural student college attendance at predominantly White colleges and universities. The elimination of the long-held "separate but equal" doctrine required higher education to open its doors to students of color and to provide equal opportunity in education. The 1954 *Brown v. Board of Education* decision destroyed sanctioned segregation in education and called into question all other facets of American life that supported racial exclusion. The *Brown* decision heralded a period of unprecedented change in American history, not the least of which occurred in higher education. After centuries of exclusion from the rights and privileges afforded White American students, Frederick Douglass' abolitionist era observation that "Power concedes nothing without a demand" (Bennett, 1984, p. 161) was manifested by widespread insistence among students of color demanding access to higher education. The history of such protest documents unrest well before the *Brown* decision among Black students enrolled at Historically Black Colleges and Universities (HBCUs), who questioned the type of education they were receiving and the status quo of Southern tradition. In the post-*Brown* era, however, students of color at predominantly White colleges and universities protested both quietly and loudly, and sometimes violently, for the right to participate in the educational advantages that are prerequisites to success in American society.

Discontent with discrimination started a national movement that was overarching in nature, seeking societal change and its resulting freedoms. Student protest during the 1960s was a dynamic phenomenon that changed the character and momentum of the civil rights movement (Exum, 1985). The philosophical changes in society extended naturally onto the college campus. The number of Black college students grew from 600,000 in 1965, most of them at HBCUs, to 1.2 million in 1980 with just 20% of that number attending HBCUs (Wilson, 1994). Latino and Asian-American student enrollments also increased, but to a lesser extent during this same period. Reportedly, dramatic increases among those student populations can be traced to the early to mid-1970s. The increase in Latino student numbers was a natural outgrowth of the revolutionary movements occurring within the Latino population, led largely by young people. The struggle for freedom by Blacks was a guide, and at times a mirror, for rallying Latinos. This was also true for Asian Americans. The shift in enrollment was accompanied by a shift in focus among student protesters from changing society and its traditions to changing the university.

Campus Responses to the Emergence of New Populations

The response of institutions to activism by students of color and their allies was indeed significant. First among the responses was the task of addressing the issue of access to higher education for populations historically underrepresented in colleges and universities. At many predominately White institutions, this period signaled the creation of recruitment and admission programs specifically targeting individuals from these groups. These efforts included the hiring of staff whose responsibilities would be devoted solely to this function and the design of financial-aid packages and admission policies to support the enrollment of students from economically disadvantaged households.

With the increased presence of students of color on college campuses, both academic and environmental issues quickly became critical. The college curriculum itself took center stage as the focal point of heated debate between college officials and students over its focus and relevance. Students of color charged that the curriculum was both narrow and mono-cultural and failed to provide course offerings that examined the history, culture, and contributions of racial and ethnic groups that had been virtually ignored by the academy. In time, many institutions responded to these charges by creating ethnic studies programs and by establishing similarly themed cultural centers and institutes.

The curricular concerns of students, however, went beyond just *what* was being taught to *who* was providing the instruction. Students demanded a more racially and ethnically diverse faculty, who could provide them with much-needed role models and mentors. Some institutions have been more successful than others in responding to the need to increase the numbers of faculty of color. Even today, effectively addressing this issue is a methodical work in progress at many colleges and universities.

As a critical mass of students of color began to emerge on campuses across the country, environmental and student support issues came to the fore as well. Students demanded social and cultural outlets more in line with their life experiences to cope with the "culture shock" many of them faced. Additionally, support programs were sought to address both the academic and social problems they confronted in what many described as hostile and isolating environments. Institutional responses to these concerns included the creation of and financial support for culturally based student organizations, special housing arrangements based on race, ethnicity, and other culturally based themes, the creation of offices or departments of "minority" affairs, specialized orientation programs, tutoring, and other academic assistance programs. To address the hostile environment issue expressed by students of color, some institutions responded by establishing "speech codes" to regulate language found to be offensive in a diverse and multicultural environment. Many colleges and universities have sponsored diversity training programs for members of their respective campus communities as another response to environmental issues and to assist with managing the changing demographics of their institutions.

Affirmative Action: A Continuing Response

Historically, legislation has resulted in both progress and setbacks in educational opportunity for diverse students. Affirmative action legislation following the civil rights era has kept the question of diversity alive on the college campus and continues to remind institutions that equal opportunity is a valuable American ideal. Affirmative action policies created to redress past discrimination by ensuring the participation of underrepresented Americans in education, business, and the workplace, have been widely and, at times, bitterly, debated in our society. While supporters of affirmative action in higher education see it as a necessary remedy to redress past discrimination, its opponents view it as discriminatory and undemocratic.

The 1978 *Bakke* decision (*Regents of the University of California v. Bakke*) was the first landmark legal decision addressing affirmative action policies at colleges and universities. In that case, the Supreme Court recognized diversity as a worthy goal in higher education, but in murky and seemingly contradictory language left its intent open to debate. In the mid- to late 1990s, affirmative action policies in higher education were again challenged in both courts and legislatures. California's Proposition 209 (Kidder, Serrano, & Ancheta, 2004), the *Hopwood* decision (*Hopwood v. Texas*, 1996) in Texas, and the "One Florida" initiative (McLemee, 2004) have all sought to eliminate state policies established to create diverse student populations.

More recently, however, the issue of affirmative action and its role in the college admissions process landed squarely in the lap of our nation's highest court once more as a result of two law suits filed against the University of Michigan, one directed at its undergraduate admission policy (*Gratz v. Bollinger*, 2003) and the other challenging the constitutionality of its law school's admissions formula (*Grutter v. Bollinger*, 2003). On June 23, 2003, the Supreme Court rendered clarifying decisions regarding the two cases and the issue of race-conscious admissions policies. In a 6 to 3 vote, the justices struck down the university's undergraduate admissions policy, which used a point-based system for applicants, automatically giving 20 points to Black applicants. But in a 5 to 4 vote, the Court upheld the law school's admissions policy, which used a less mechanical admissions formula but still favored underrepresented applicants. Of particular importance in this case is the Court's agreement with Justice Powell's earlier 1978 *Bakke* opinion that "student body diversity is a compelling state interest that can justify the use of race in university admissions" (American Council on Education, 2003, p. 2). Furthermore, the majority in *Grutter* found that diversity in higher education has "substantial" benefits, specifically citing that "diversity breaks down stereotypes, invigorates classroom discussion, and helps prepare students to work in a diverse economy" (American Council on Education, 2003, p. 2).

Although qualified support for affirmative action was provided by the 2003 decisions, a series of new questions has arisen, making it clear that new challenges to affirmative action should be anticipated. Critics and dissenting justices have posed questions such as whether it is proper for the university to have a role in determining the racial composition of the nation's leadership class, whether race is, in fact, an appropriate factor in determining diversity, whether social class should be used instead of race, and whether individuality is being preserved as a part of the admissions picture. These questions and others that are sure to arise indicate a nation continuing to grapple with its responsibility to implement the ideal of equal opportunity. An added dimension when considering affirmative action involves a perceptual change many students have expressed in the way they want to be treated by colleges and universities. At a time when academic qualifications and achievements are more in question, some students of color want to be acknowledged but don't want to be separated from White students for fear of being viewed as deficient or less deserving of educational opportunities. The overall impact of the Court's decision on the demographic make-up of our campuses has yet to be fully seen. As the impact becomes apparent, we will see continuing student activism requiring campuses to become more responsive to the needs of the student populations they must serve.

Demographics: The Changing Nature of Our Student Population

Bogue and Aper (2000) observed, "The story of increased access and diversity in American college students must be counted as one of the most dramatic changes in the profile of American higher education" (p. 139). Dramatic indeed. At no other period in the history of higher education has such a diverse range of participants characterized the American collegian. This diversity not only reflects the increased representation of students from various racial and ethnic groups, but also includes other student populations whose presence have, at some level, affected institutional policies, programs, conversations on diversity, and the nature of demands for student freedoms. This drastic demographic shift presents both opportunities and challenges to college and university leaders as they attempt to effectively navigate the sometimes tricky waters inherent in managing a multicultural environment.

One of the most noticeable reversals in college enrollment trends is in the area of gender representation. For the past several years, female students have constituted a majority of undergraduate students. Another notable change can be found when examining the economic backgrounds of students. College, reserved for the financially elite, is now either the aspiration or the expectation for persons from a wide range of socioeconomic backgrounds. And what of age diversity? Beginning with the influx of WWII veterans, adults have been going to college in record numbers for decades. While many still cling to the popular image of college students as traditional 18- to 24-year-olds, others have recognized and facilitated the influx of returning adults to higher education. Diversity certainly also extends to the more than 10% of all college students who identify as gay, lesbian, or bisexual (Evans, Forney, & Guido-DiBrito, 1998). The presence of diverse students highlights the importance of integrating relevant content into the curriculum, hosting student organizations and support groups, and developing programs that offer a means for supportive faculty and staff to help create an environment in which these populations can explore more aspects of their identity and increase their level of self-awareness (Hamrick, Evans, & Schuh, 2002).

Another group now included in the dialogue on diversity consists of disabled students. As a result of the passage of federal nondiscrimination laws over the years, particularly the Americans with Disabilities Act (Upcraft,

Gardner, & Barefoot, 2005) and the Rehabilitation Act (Upcraft & Gardner, 1989), institutions have been required to pay closer attention to students with these needs. For colleges and universities receiving federal funds, mandates ensure equal access to educational programs and activities for disabled students attending such institutions. Additionally, at a time when the nation has a heightened awareness of international issues, religious and international diversity issues have gained increased attention on campus. The breadth and depth of student diversity have made the questions we currently face very different than if we were solely addressing racial and ethnic differences. Often diverse groups coalesce, understanding their commonalities and using them to strengthen their calls for increased student freedoms.

Traditionally defined diverse students (Blacks, Latinos, Asians, and Native Americans) remain a growing presence on our college campuses. Included are Asian student populations, whose origins can be traced to more than 30 countries in Asia and Pacific Rim nations; Native American students from more than 500 federally recognized tribes; Latino students whose origins are in 20 Spanish-speaking countries, in addition to those who do not speak Spanish but ethnically identify as Latino; and Black students whose origins are traced to the many countries of Africa and the Caribbean (Brown & Rivas, 1995). While enrollment patterns for some of these groups have seesawed over the past few decades, their overall participation rate is significant, and their effect important. Adding to this multicultural milieu is the recent emergence of students from multiracial and multiethnic backgrounds. Cortes (2000) addresses the issues faced by those students who choose to "honor the roles that each part of their heritage plays in shaping their personal sense of being and reject the idea that they must choose a single racial identity" (p. 7). Race, ethnicity, gender, age, religion, disability, class, and sexual orientation are all characteristics of diversity on today's college campuses. College and university professionals must expect that student freedom will continue to encompass these increasing multiple identities and must be prepared to adapt to the changing needs and demands of an increasingly diverse student population.

What Lies Ahead?

Looking back at how colleges and universities have historically responded to student demonstrations and protest, the word *reactive* immediately comes to mind. Today's campuses, however, have the opportunity to be much more proactive in responding to these areas, particularly those relating to issues of diversity and multiculturalism. Unlike the pre-1960 period where the numbers of students of color on college campuses were so few that college officials focused solely on issues of race, diversity on today's campuses includes innumerable differences in race, ethnicity, national origin, gender, age, class, sexual orientation, disability, and religion. Even for campuses that persist in a racially oriented view of diversity, the significant differences among members of any individual racial group make it difficult and often impossible to develop comprehensive programmatic solutions.

Institutions seeking a proactive approach to campus diversity should consider the following suggestions:

Create and Implement an Institution-Wide Strategic Plan That Addresses Both the Short- and Long-Term Impact of Diversity Issues

Diversity has been actualized on campus through the development of new curricula, enrollment initiatives, support programs including financial aid, and training efforts. While gains have been made in certain areas, a holistic view of the impact of these demographic, cultural, academic and social changes can assist us in responding to student needs before problems erupt. Based on feedback received from campuses asked to evaluate the success of their respective diversity initiatives, the authors of *To Form a More Perfect Union: Campus Diversity Initiatives* (Garcia et al., 1999) offer advice to institutions seeking to implement more effective, single-delivery diversity projects, as well as more comprehensive diversity initiatives. Their recommendations include specific suggestions in the six following areas: (1) institutionalizing diversity initiatives, (2) building consensus and communicating results, (3) engaging faculty, (4) developing students within the classroom, (5) linking student affairs and academic affairs, and (6) sustaining the value of networking. Such an approach can provide campuses with the necessary framework to build diversity into strategic planning and institutional goal-setting while being sensitive to issues of student freedoms that could potentially arise.

Adapt Institutional Support Services to Address Intragroup Differences

Institutions should be aware of the within-group demographic diversity of their student populations so that they can provide programs and services that are tailored to the specific origins and experiences of those groups. For example, programs for Asian students must recognize the immense language, national, and class diversity that exists within these populations. No single culturally oriented program could effectively address all students in this group. Colleges and universities have a responsibility be informed about their student populations through research and assessment in order to adequately adapt instructional, academic, and social support services for students.

Anticipate and Manage the Likely Tensions That Will Occur as a Result of the Increasing Socioeconomic Diversity Among our Students

The socioeconomic backgrounds of today's college students represents a much wider range of income levels than in previous decades. With the ever-rising costs of higher education, student activism surrounding issues of access and affordability, particularly at public colleges and universities, will certainly need to be addressed by institutions. Colleges and universities can proactively conduct a comprehensive review and assessment of their financial-aid programs and policies, as well as their methodology for determining financial-aid awards and the setting of tuition/room and board fees.

As appropriate to their institutional culture, colleges and universities may consider any or all of the following in addressing this area:

- Utilize data on the socioeconomic background of matriculated students in the development of institutional financial-aid policies.

- Make efforts to inform students of the intricacies involved in the financial-aid process, the role of governmental agencies in the awarding of state or federal aid programs, and lobbying/advocacy opportunities available to students.

- Provide continual institutional financial support for specific programs that serve economically disadvantaged students.

- Establish student representation on financial-aid advisory boards or councils.

Additionally, natural emotional tension can result for students at both ends of the socioeconomic spectrum when they become members of the same community but have access to different types of resources. Institutions should include socioeconomic diversity in campus programming that promotes awareness and understanding of student differences and similarities.

Provide Appropriate Programs and Services That Address the Characteristics and Needs of Older Students

The older or returning student in higher education comprises a significant portion of the U.S. college student demographic. Surveys, phone interviews, and focus groups directed at this population can provide campuses with valuable information regarding their educational and social needs. Where appropriate, campuses should include the voices of these students in discussions of student services and other issues that impact their campus experience and potential student freedoms. Characteristics attributed to this group—a more focused, consumer-oriented approach to academic pursuits, as well as high expectations of the collegiate experience—necessitate the delivery of programs and services that address the age, commuter status, personal priorities, time restrictions and part-time attendance of these individuals.

Be Sensitive to the Diversity of Religious Beliefs and Cultural Practices

How are campus communities affected when the religious beliefs and cultural practices of students are viewed with suspicion and guilt by association? It is important that campuses recognize the "teachable moment" when campus misunderstandings occur. Institutions can respond effectively by supporting student freedom of expression and providing educational opportunities for open dialogue and information-sharing among student groups. Providing advisement and programming opportunities to religious and cultural organizations offers institutional support for their existence and encourages a safe environment for all students. A possible organizational support for religious organizations might be the establishment of a campus board or council that unifies them under a common, though diverse, spiritual bond. Lastly, conflict resolution and mediation training for campus personnel and student organizational leaders can serve as an invaluable tool when tensions arise.

Truly Listen to What Diverse Student Populations Are Asking for in Their Letters, E-mails, Vigils, Rallies, Marches, and Other Forms of Activism; Have Campus Protocols in Place to Address Student Concerns

In many cases of student activism, the threat of danger and classroom disruption keeps administrators caught in the moment. But a look just below the surface often reveals important information about the way dissenting students internalize the learning environment in which they are enrolled. A close examination of these various forms of protest and the motivations behind them can lead to knowledge, awareness, and change that can positively affect the college experience for all students. Additionally, campuses should examine whether they are prepared to face student demands for increased freedom by the processes and protocols they have in place. Are students aware of the campus resources for advocacy? Are they aware of campus policies regarding dissent? Are campus policies related to discrimination and bias clear and understandable? Campuses should establish pathways to resolution that serve as a clearly communicated system of response for student concerns.

Diversity on the nation's college campuses has challenged the university's ability to synthesize legal interpretation with institutional policies and practices, while taking fairness into consideration. We have only addressed some of the pivotal questions colleges and universities must address in order to satisfactorily include new voices in the academy. As we continually strive to accept, assist, and understand the broad array of students we now call diverse, we are also aware that each new day brings with it new calls for greater and more inclusive student freedoms.

References

American Council on Education. (2003, September). *Affirmative action in higher education after Grutter v. Bollinger and Gratz v. Bollinger* (pp. 1-2). Washington, DC: Hogan & Hartson, L.L.P.

Arthur, J. & Schapiro, A. (Eds.). (1995). Affirmative action in universities: Regents of the University of California v. Bakke. In *Campus wars: Multiculturalism and the politics of difference* (pp. 137-143). Boulder, CO: Westview Press.

Anyaso, H. (Ed.). (2003, December 18). Black issues in higher education; The legal survival of race in college admissions. *Year in Review, 20*(22), 26.

Bennett, L., Jr. (1984) *Before the Mayflower: A history of Black America.* (5th ed.). New York: Penguin.

Bogue, G. E. & Aper, J. (2000). *Exploring the heritage of American higher education: The evolution of philosophy and policy.* The American Council on Education Oryx Press series on higher education. Phoenix, AZ: Oryx Press.

Cortes, C. (2000). The diversity within: Intermarriage, identity, and campus community. *About Campus, 5*(1), 5-10.

Evans, N., Forney, D., & Guido-DiBrito, F. (Eds.). (1998). *Student development in college: Theory, research, and practice.* San Francisco: Jossey-Bass.

Exum, W. H. (1985). *Paradoxes of protest.* Philadelphia: Temple University Press.

Fleming, J. (1984). *Blacks in college.* San Francisco: Jossey Bass.

Fox, G. (1996). *Hispanic nation: Culture, politics, and the constructing of identity.* Tucson, AZ: University of Arizona Press.

Garcia, M., Hudgins, A., Musil, C., Nettles, M., Sedlacek, W., & Smith, D. (1999). *To form a more perfect union: Campus diversity initiatives* (pp. 33-39). Washington, DC: Association of American Colleges and Universities.

Green, M. F. (Ed.). (1989). *Minorities on campus: A handbook for enhancing diversity.* Washington, DC: American Council on Education.

Hamrick, F., Evans, N., & Schuh, J. (Eds.). (2002). *Foundations of student affairs practice*. San Francisco: Jossey-Bass.

Justiz, M., Wilson, R., & Bjork, L. (Eds). (1994). *Minorities in higher education*. American Council on Education Oryx Press series on higher education. Phoenix, AZ: Oryx Press.

Kidder, W., Serrano, S., & Ancheta, A. (2004, May 21). In California, a misguided battle over race. *The Chronicle of Higher Education, 50*(37), B16.

Kidwell, C. S. (1994). Higher education issues in Native-American communities. In M. J. Justiz, R. Wilson, & L. G. Bjork (Eds.), *Minorities in higher education* (pp. 240-258). Phoenix, AZ: Oryx Press.

Lemann, N. (2003, June 29). Ideas & trends: Beyond Bakke; A decision that universities can relate to. *The New York Times*, p. 14.

McCune, P. (2001). What do disabilities have to do with diversity? *About Campus, 6*(2), 5-12.

McLemee, S. (2004, July 2). Florida court dismisses NAACP suit. *The Chronicle of Higher Education, 50*(43), A22.

Schmidt. P. (2003, November 28). Academe's Hispanic future. *The Chronicle of Higher Education, L*(14), A8-16.

Smith, D. G. (1989). *The challenge of diversity: Involvement or alienation in the academy?* (Report No. 5). Washington, DC: The George Washington University, School of Education and Human Development.

Steinberg, J. (2003, June 24). The Supreme Court: University admissions; an admissions guide. *The New York Times*, p. 1.

Upcraft, M. L., Gardner, J. N., & Associates. (1989). *The freshman year experience* (p. 345). San Francisco: Jossey-Bass.

Upcraft, M. L., Gardner, J. N., Barefoot, B., & Associates. (2005). *Challenging & supporting the first-year student* (p. 20). San Francisco: Jossey-Bass.

Washington, M. (1996). The minority student in college: A historical analysis. In C. Turner, M. Garcia, A. Nora, & L. I. Rendon (Eds.), *Racial & ethnic diversity in higher education*. ASHE Reader Series. Needham Heights, MA.: Simon & Shuster Custom Publishing.

Wilson, R. (1994). The participation of African Americans in American higher education. In M. Justiz, R. Wilson, & L. Bjork (Eds), *Minorities in higher education*. American Council on Education/Oryx Press series on higher education (pp. 195-209). Phoenix, AZ: Oryx Press.

Wright, B. (1989). For the children of infidels?: American Indian education in the colonial colleges. In L. F. Goodchild & H. S. Wechsler (Eds.), *The history of higher education* (pp. 53-59). ASHE Reader Series. Needham, MA: Simon & Schuster Custom Publishing.

Wright, D. J. (Ed.) (1987). *Responding to the needs of today's minority students.* San Francisco: Jossey Bass.

Chapter 5

International Dimensions of Student Freedom

Sabine U. O'Hara

The student movement of the 1960s and '70s, which included demands for freedom and reform, antiwar protests, human rights demonstrations and social change agendas, was heard loud and clear not only in the United States but also on European college campuses. And many dimensions of its impact both in the United States and Europe are still with us today despite the fact that it has long since been replaced by a quieter and less polarized student body. In Germany, for example, academic garb is no longer worn at graduation, convocation, or other official ceremonies. *"Unter den Talaren der Muff von tausend Jahren"*—under the robes the stench of a thousand years—was one of the slogans of students who challenged long-standing German university traditions, definitions, and privileges. While the most turbulent years of the student movement in Germany were over by the mid 1970s, its impact continued in student protests against nuclear energy and nuclear waste storage, the arms race, and foreign policy throughout the 1970s and early '80s.

By the mid 1980s, things had become pretty quiet on college and university campuses in Europe and the United States. In comparing college experiences in the United States and in Germany, based on an admittedly small, personal sample on both sides of the Atlantic Ocean, some differences emerge.[1] U.S. students appear to be far less argumentative, far more non-confrontational, apolitical, and conformist than their German counterparts, who consider a heated debate both a given on a college campus and an expression of personal and academic freedoms. Yet even so, there was relative calm on college campuses throughout the 1990s both in the U.S. and in Europe.

---

[1] The author was born and educated in Germany and received her doctorate in environmental economics from the University of Göttingen, Germany. Since 1984 she has lived and worked in the United States at colleges and universities on the east coast and in the Midwest.

And what about today? Given recent news reports, the calmest of times may well be over. Europe's universities are struggling with the implications of the Bologna protocols of 1999 (The European Higher Education Area, 1999). According to these agreements, European universities will undergo significant changes by 2012 in an effort to unify Europe's educational models and policies. The diverse landscape of school systems and university systems within the member countries of the European Union is scheduled to undergo unification efforts similar to those in agricultural, trade, economics, labor policies and currencies. One of the aims of these unification efforts appears to be the adoption of a U.S.-style system with its baccalaureate and graduate level degrees. This means significant changes for some of Europe's university systems, that have distinct general and college preparatory school systems through Grade 13 and lead directly into a specialized university education. The global market, a key argument of the Bologna agreements, demands such changes and would benefit from a global education system. Some of Europe's current educational systems simply take too long and are not responsive enough to market demand.

Yet the Bologna agreements alone do not appear to be what causes the German university community to be in protest mode again. Students, faculty, and administrators are marching in the streets once again, but this time together. Today's protests are directed toward the significant cuts in financial support of German universities in light of the government's struggles to close a looming budget deficit and address the staggering costs of German reunification. Budget cuts and reorganization initiatives have also been at the root of protests at Austrian Universities (Labi, 2003). And budget cuts have also brought some comparatively small groups of U.S. students to the streets, as public colleges and universities across the country have announced double-digit tuition hikes in the wake of state deficits from New York to California.

The core messages of these protests, though, seem to be somewhat different than those of the earlier student protests. U.S. students call for a curtailment of costs that will maintain access to a college education for less affluent students, a social justice agenda one might say. German protests take a somewhat broader view. At least for the time being, German universities do not charge tuition. Education has long been free and is generally viewed as an investment in the future. Yet lack of public support and pressure to shift funding to the private sector have sparked broader discussions about educational quality, the independence of research from commercial interests, and the country's commitment to investing in its future through education rather than defense spending.

Some of these messages do indeed sound reminiscent of the 1960s and '70s student protests and their call for freedom of expression, peace, and an end to the war in Vietnam. And indeed, our global political landscape provides much material for discussion and demonstration on today's college campuses. The wars in Iraq and Afghanistan, conflict in the Middle East, and turmoil in several African nations all remind us of the fragility of our global web. If one follows some of the recent rhetoric in the United States surrounding the Iraq conflict, there can be little doubt that the ghost of the Vietnam era is present. Protests abroad brought hundreds of thousands of people to the streets in opposition to the war in Iraq. Protests on college campuses and in many of our cities here in the United States, particularly prior to the start of the conflict, called for peace and for an end to violence over oil.

And there is another theme that is reminiscent of the 1960s and '70s student protests. The recent legal challenge to Michigan's admissions policies made it abundantly clear that race relations on U.S. campuses are far from resolved (Greenhouse, 2003). The recent ruling, that race can be a legitimate factor in public college and university admissions, will no doubt continue to spark discussion about equal opportunity, equal access, and diversity (Greenhouse, 2003).

So have we come full circle? Are we currently revisiting the themes and issues that sparked the student protests of the 1960s and '70s here in the United States and in Europe? To some extent,. We are still concerned about a domestic and a global agenda of human rights, economic justice, opportunity, the protection of civil liberties and freedom. Yet today's protests are far more carefully delineated and less wide spread. *No* to the war in Iraq, but *yes* to supporting our troops appears to be a common and careful framing of antiwar protests. Similarly, recent surveys of British protesters indicated their antipathy with the war in Iraq and their sympathy for the American people. And just as our involvement in a war on the Asian continent galvanized the student movement of more than 30 years ago here and abroad, so it may well be U.S. foreign affairs that remind us anew of our yearning for freedom, peace, and justice, particularly at a time when we have become keenly aware how much our lives as global citizens are connected to events and people abroad. We do, after all, live in a post-9-11 world that confronts those of us living in the United States in new ways with our connectedness as citizens of one world.

Yet there is another dimension to the freedom past student protests sought that may well be even more important than a revisiting of past themes. The question, particularly for United States colleges and universities, is how do we need to educate our students to be and become global citizens? How do we raise global awareness and increase multicultural literacy? Are we doing enough and are we doing the right kinds of things, particularly in light of the leadership role of the United States in world affairs? U.S. students do not have the same exposure to other cultures as their European counterparts. Secondary schools have continuously reduced foreign language requirements and students' exposure to foreign countries and peoples happens more by accident rather than by design.

At the same time, we enjoy unprecedented levels of freedom of international movement, travel and study. This unprecedented mobility is evident in our college catalogues and on our campuses. Virtually every U.S. college and university offers study abroad opportunities. International education has become a common criterion by which colleges are evaluated. Some colleges even require their students to get an international/multicultural education experience, in the form of either study abroad or curricular requirements in cultural awareness and diversity. Yet the nagging question persists, whether the unprecedented level of freedom of movement and the growth in international education experiences that U.S. colleges and universities offer are assets that we use well or resources that we squander. Do we contribute to international understanding and cultural awareness? Do we simply prepare our students to advance U.S. interests in global markets? Do we contribute to misunderstanding and the perpetuation of prejudice? Is all this talk about cultural awareness simply irrelevant anyway in an increasingly homogeneous global marketplace? Or are our markets not as homogeneous after all (O'Hara & Biesecker, 2004)?[2] In other words, do we use the opportunities our freedom affords us to develop ties and better understandings of each other, or do we simply remain spectators? Are we more interested in having others learn about us than we in learning about them? The unprecedented freedom and access to travel we enjoy in the U.S. is certainly not commonplace. For citizens of many other countries, particularly in the southern hemisphere, travel is a luxury reserved only for the wealthy; millions encounter foreign lands and other cultures, but as refugees rather than travelers.

And does our freedom matter? Can we make a difference as educators? The answer is clearly yes. It matters whether or not we are aware of others. Some understanding of other people's cultural norms, religious, social, economic, and political beliefs, demographic conditions, and worldviews does matter. The shock of 9-11 and its aftermath should certainly have taught us that we cannot afford to be ignorant about others or their opinions of us. Even the less dramatic lessons we may have learned in our commonplace economic and political interactions should have made us aware of the need to be informed and knowledgeable about others' customs and experiences. One of the core commitments of U.S. liberal arts education has traditionally been to prepare students to become responsible citizens. In today's world this must necessarily mean a commitment to preparing students to be global citizens (see, for example, Cornwell & Stoddard, 1999). This requires that students be exposed to different viewpoints and their respective cultural, social, economic, religious and gender perspectives that invariably contribute to forming a particular worldview (see, for example, Segovia & Tolbert, 1995). Despite the long held

---

[2] A special issue of the *Review of Social Economy* (2003) explores the question whether the impact of globalization and European unification undermines or preserves the specific characteristics of the economies and social policies of E.U. member countries.

assumptions of Western thought, neither our cultural perspectives nor the perspective of Kuhnian normal science are objective, value-neutral, or universal. Instead they represent a particular subjectivity. Its critique was precisely one of the aims of the student movement of 35 years ago.

And there can be no doubt that we have learned much about, if not from, our international connections during these past 30 years. U.S. students and faculty travel to Europe and Asia, Africa and Latin America, and the fastest growing destination in recent years, Australia (Koh Chin, 2003) We know how to embed international experiences into our curriculum. We offer co-op and internship experiences abroad and many U.S. colleges have overseas partners in education and the private sector. Yet, despite our growing experience, many have raised questions about the learning outcomes of our international education programs. One could argue, no doubt, that any study-abroad opportunity is valuable. Any opportunity to travel broadens our horizon, gets us in touch with history, confronts us with strange foods, unfamiliar ways of doing things, and unknown places. And yet, travel abroad may or may not succeed in allowing us to reflect on who we are and who the (w)holy other is whom we meet in these foreign lands. Yet, do we really provide opportunities for learning that open the minds and hearts of our students, or are the learning opportunities we provide more likely to keep them (and us) focused on ourselves, on confirming our own perspectives, and on preserving our advantages and biases? In other words, do the opportunities we offer our students maintain their and our comfort zones or do they challenge us and make us feel uncomfortable?

Challenging comfort zones, challenging the familiar, questioning established norms and assumptions, these were certainly some of the hallmarks of the 1960s student movement. Its claim was precisely a claim to freedom from established norms: the freedom to speak, to confront, and to do things differently. Some of its questioning and moving beyond familiar comfort zones actually manifested itself in both literal and figurative excursions into other, particularly eastern, cultures.

A term that has come to connote the kind of exposure to discomfort that challenges our own mindsets and perceptions is the term *immersion*.

Immersion implies engagement, active experience, contact with local culture and people. The hoped-for result is an opening up beyond one's own boundaries quite different from the observer attitude of the tourist or the distanced scientist. Language certainly plays an important role in facilitating immersion experiences, and it seems unfortunate that the commitment to language learning in U.S. high schools and colleges is in decline even as we confront the downside of our limited language facility in business and foreign policy. Learning other languages does more than facilitate communication. It gives us a sense of how others frame the world, frame their experience of reality, frame their values of human and nonhuman relationships. And yet language is not the only approach to immersion. Virtually every discipline has a role to play. There is the study of political science, formal and informal institutions, and differences in institutional arrangements; and of the impact trade patterns have on local economies; the tensions between local and global economies; and national and foreign business practices. There is the experience of cultural practices and social systems, the challenge posed by our shrinking pool of biological diversity, and the need for virtually every country on the globe to wrestle with water management issues. A commitment to immersion is a truly multidisciplinary endeavor. Yes, language may be a barrier to immersion, but there are also the barriers of submitting to local notions of time, of being served rather than serving, of accepting local priorities rather than defining the agenda.

Freedom of expression and freedom from constraints, these were some of the key concepts the student movement of the 1960s stood for. These freedoms invariably require that we reflect on our own place in the world, on our relationship to others, and on our own presuppositions and perceptions. By moving ever closer together as a global community, linked by global communication networks, transportation systems, and economic interactions and dependencies, we again are challenged to reflect on our expressions and constraints as well as our freedoms. Despite our global connections, we also remain part of local and regional communities with their own distinctive spatial, climatic, social, and cultural characteristics and ways of thinking and acting. Claiming and exercising our own freedoms cannot come at the expense of others, achieved through mindsets of imperialism and superiority where some invariably win and others loose. And it cannot be achieved by allowing secular and religious fundamentalism to limit our scope of inquiry and discourse. Instead its requires that we are open to learning from each others' strengths and weaknesses, open to debate, open to defining our own standpoint and allowing others to define theirs, and open to living with differences (O'Hara, 1999).

Can we learn to use our unprecedented freedom of communication and movement to advance our global community? Can we become informed global citizens and preserve and even celebrate our diversity? We have certainly come to realize the need to preserve our biological diversity as a source for pharmaceutical progress, medical advances, and future food security. But our social and cultural diversity too are under duress and deserve attention. By social and cultural diversity I mean "the diverse ways of social and economic arrangements by which peoples have organized their societies, particularly the underlying assumptions, goals, values, and social behaviors guiding these arrangements and processes" (O'Hara, 1995, p. 31). Just as in the case of biodiversity, we may come to realize that diversity may be a key in adapting, in coping with pressures, and in finding new solutions. Thus, it will require more than a revisiting of past themes to truly advance our freedom and to offer our students a chance to live in a peaceful, just, and sustainable world.

References

Cornwell, G. & Stoddard, E. (1999). *Globalizing knowledge: Connecting international and intercultural studies.* Washington, DC: Association of American Colleges and Universities.

The European Higher Education Area. (1999). The Bologna declaration of 19 June, 1999. *Joint declaration of the European ministers of education.* Brussels, Belgium.

Greenhouse, L. (2003, June 24). Justices back affirmative action by 5 to 4, but wider vote bans a racial point system. *The New York Times*, p. A23.

Koh Chin, H-K. (Ed.). (2003) *Open door: Report on international education exchange.* New York: Institute of International Education.

Labi, A. (2003, December 19). Across western Europe, students protest plans to increase tuition. *The Chronicle of Higher Education, 50*(17), A40.

O'Hara, S. (1995). Valuing socio-diversity. *International Journal of Social Economics, 22*(5), 31-49.

O'Hara, S. (1999). Economics, ecology and quality of life: Who Evaluates? *Feminist Economics, 5*(2), 83-89.

O'Hara, S. & Biesecker, A. (2004). Globalization: Homogenization of newfound diversity? *Review of Social Economy, LXI*(3), 281-294.

Review of Social Economy. (September 2003) *LXI*(3).

Segovia, F. & Tolbert, M. (1995). *Reading from place: Vol. I & II.* Minneapolis, MN: Fortress Press

Chapter 6

Contemporary Issues in the Constitutional Rights of Students in American Higher Education

William B. Werner

The student protests, demonstrations, and activism of the 1960s and '70s grew out of, and themselves generated, issues that were as many and diverse as the students themselves. But among all the causes advanced by college students in that age, one that served to unify their interests perhaps more than any other was their demand for the fundamental right to protest in the first place. Students' legal rights on campus were much less certain then than they are today, and many campus administrators responded to student protests and demonstrations by exercising what was generally thought to be the absolute lawful right to regulate and restrain student conduct on campus.

This approach, while supported by the state of the law at that time, drew an indignant and forceful reaction from the students, and connected many of them to a central theme—the deprivation of their constitutional rights to assemble peaceably and speak freely. This issue connected college students nationwide not only with each other but also with the larger civil rights movement, perhaps drawing some additional public sympathy to their cause and, at the least, providing a moral and constitutional basis for their activities and ideals.

These connections, however strong or effective they may have been, were short-lived, since by 1973 the U.S. Supreme Court in a series of related cases had firmly declared that college students, at least those attending public institutions, retain all of their constitutional civil rights on campus, most importantly their rights to free speech and assembly. The early cases were monumental victories for the students and erected sturdy legal barriers to the efforts of campus administrators and others to curb or prevent otherwise lawful speech, protests, and demonstrations. While borderline cases such as office sit-ins and disruptive behavior continued to produce difficult legal questions, by the mid-1970s the fundamental rights of the students to speak freely, to assemble, and to protest on campus were no longer in doubt. While the protests and demonstrations continued under their new legal protection, the students' early and decisive legal victories diminished their common ground with the national civil rights movement.

Whatever the ultimate effects of those legal battles on student activism and freedom, however, the constitutional victories themselves were landmark in American legal history. The recognition of the students' constitutional rights on campus implicated a multitude of potential issues, from First Amendment rights to the guarantees of equal protection and due process of law. An exhaustive account of the constitutional rights of students in all their permutations would likely command several volumes; this chapter is limited to two of the most significant issues that remain problematic today: (a) the impact of campus speech codes on First Amendment rights, and (b) the conflict between the students' right to religious freedom and the prohibition of state support or establishment of religion.

It must be noted at the outset that this chapter addresses primarily the rights of students of public universities. While the leadership of private institutions may be equally concerned for the civil freedoms of their students, the legal basis for constitutional protection discussed in this chapter derives from the fundamental legal equivalence of the state and the state-run university. Constitutional protections are generally not applicable, at least in a legal sense, on a privately funded and operated university campus. Nonetheless, the basic civil rights of students raise compelling moral and philosophical issues that are arguably important to all forms of higher education, but are beyond the scope of this chapter.

Also, although the cases discussed in this chapter arose in higher education settings, it bears mentioning that there is little constitutional distinction between college and secondary public school students. Research in the area of student rights will reveal that most of the rulings that are applied to higher education cases actually arose in grade school and high school contexts. In fact, the first U.S. Supreme Court case to address the issue of students' civil rights was in a case filed against a public high school (*Tinker v. Des Moines Independent School District*, 1969). The federal courts have yet to recognize any meaningful distinction in the context of civil rights between students at different levels of public education. In the opinions of some commentators recently, this represents a failure in American constitutional law to acknowledge an important changing reality—that the vast majority of college students are now adults, at least by the legal definition (Silversten, 2000, p. 1295).

The University as State Actor

When *Student Freedom in American Higher Education* (Vaccaro & Covert, 1969) was published, the body of law applicable to higher education administration was influenced heavily by the now infamous doctrine of in loco parentis. Under this doctrine, educational institutions of all sorts were held to have parental responsibility and, thus by necessity, absolute authority "in place of the parents" over the conduct of students, both on and off campus. Although the legal basis for the doctrine was always somewhat tenuous, it was generally understood or at least believed that the institution, as an arm of the state, held exclusive constitutional power to govern itself and thus inherent discretion and authority over the students. Administrators wielded broad and nearly autonomous power in their handling of student affairs, since whatever civil rights the students may have held off campus were assumed forfeited upon entrance to the halls of academia.

In cases leading up to the late 1960s, the constitutional rights of students were gaining some recognition but were still regularly outweighed by the university administration's inherent legal authority as governor of the institution. An important constitutional underpinning of this line of law, however, was the premise that higher education was considered a privilege provided by the government to qualified citizens and not more generally a benefit of citizenship. This is a critical and often dispositive distinction in constitutional law, because a privilege may be provided unequally and revoked without due process or just cause, while a benefit comes with all the constitutional guarantees of freedom, equal protection, and due process (e.g., *Widmar v. Vincent*, 1981).

But then in the late 1960s the state and federal courts reversed field on this question and held that public education at any level is a benefit of government (e.g., *Goldberg v. Regents*, 1967). These decisions placed university administrators for the first time in the same constitutional position as police officers and other arms of the state: bound to observe the constitutional civil rights of the students and no longer having authority beyond that duty. This same decision formed part of the basis for the racial integration of public schools and universities, since the right to equal protection of the law guaranteed equal access to the benefits of citizenship.

Private colleges and universities are not state actors and thus continue to enjoy significant control over student conduct. Higher education at a private institution is neither a privilege nor a benefit of the state; it is a private relationship free of most constitutional rights and restrictions. Few private colleges and universities, however, seem to be availing themselves of their legal ability to ignore constitutional protections. Many private institutions have adopted at some time or another, either formally or informally, a policy of respecting the civil rights of students even though the rights technically do not exist in that context. This may have been one of the more important and lasting impacts of the era of campus unrest: the voluntary recognition and respect for civil rights that are typically afforded many students today even in the absence of any legal compulsion.

In the context of public higher education, however, the freedoms of college students are now situated on much more solid constitutional ground (*Healy v. James*, 1972; O'Neil, 1997). But the case of student freedom is far from closed. The boundaries of students' legal rights are regularly tested in the federal courts and a broad array of difficult constitutional issues continue to confront university administrators and the courts. Two that have gained much attention recently relate directly to fundamental student freedoms: freedom of speech and freedom of religion. Although neither is fully resolved yet, they represent two fronts on which students continue to secure and defend their constitutional civil rights.

Freedom of Hate Speech

The freedom of speech gained new respect in the midst of, or at least to some degree on account of, student activism in the 1960s and '70s. In earlier years, the halls of academia were regulated strictly at the discretion of the administrators, who allowed little deviance from standards of proper conduct and speech. But now, legal cases and journals are replete with pronouncements of the college campus as the penultimate forum for free speech and one of the last true bastions of open civic debate (Hentoff, 1992; Silversten, 2000). In some ways, we've recently reverted to earlier times. Changing social values associated with diversity and cultural sensitivity and developing liabilities for harassment and discrimination have reversed the tide on some freedoms students won only a few decades ago.

Colleges and universities have in recent years implemented or at least attempted to implement some form of campus speech code, hate speech code, or antiharassment policy. The typical code, in whatever form, prohibits speech that is intended or would reasonably be expected to harass, intimidate, or alienate others or to cause harm to others—so-called hate speech. These codes are not simply the result of changing educational diversity or social sensitivities. To a large degree, they are defensive mechanisms designed not just to protect students from verbal assault but also to protect the institution from rapidly evolving legal risks associated with diversity and social sensitivity.

Growing legal liabilities for sexual, racial, religious, and ethnic harassment and discrimination have presented campus administrators with a difficult conflict between the students' free speech rights and their protection from potentially harmful or disruptive speech. Some see the outcome of this conflict as a matter of balancing (and thus compromising) competing legal interests; others view the present state of affairs as an unwarranted double standard on the freedom of speech.

If students enjoy the same constitutional rights on campus as they do elsewhere, then it would seem that student speech on campus would be protected to the same degree as the very same speech in any other public space or forum. The right to free speech in public places is fundamental in American jurisprudence, and any attempt to regulate or restrict speech in a public place is met with the very highest standards of judicial scrutiny (e.g., *Cohen v. California*, 1971). But while the content of speech is protected, the right to free speech does not exist in a vacuum. From the standpoint of constitutional protection, all speech must be evaluated in its context and for its potential impact. One may be prohibited from shouting, "Fire!" in a crowded theatre, for example, on account of the context and likely consequences, not the content, of the speech.

The U.S. Supreme Court has rarely addressed free speech cases in the context of a college campus. It can be presumed, however, such cases will continue to be analyzed according to usual constitutional standards, by comparing the relative values of the rights in conflict and their effects, both in terms of the parties' own interests and those of society. The societal value of free speech in public places is assumed in American constitutional law and is difficult to overcome absent some imminent harm or danger to another person, such as obscenity and "fighting words" (*Cohen v. California*, 1971, p. 20). Thus, the future of campus speech codes in constitutional law will be determined largely by the judicial reaction to the university's asserted interests behind the codes: not only security and safety but also diversity, cultural sensitivity, and mounting risks of legal liability. These cases test the societal value of such goals and will ultimately turn on their perceived value in the context of higher education.

As in other areas of constitutional law, there are circumstances in which the restriction of regulation of speech is permitted. But even when the institution's legal basis for regulating speech is legitimate and substantial, its right to regulate is strictly limited to prevent any overreaching—the regulation must be tailored to prohibit only that speech that is deemed unprotected by the constitution. If a speech code is found by a court to be too vague, or to include in its prohibitions speech that is protected, then the code will be declared unconstitutional and unenforceable. The case of the one university's speech code demonstrates the difficulty of drawing that fine line.

In response to what the governing board called a "rising tide of racial intimidation and harassment on campus" (*Doe v. University of Michigan*, 1989, p. 853) in the mid-1980s, the University of Michigan adopted a new Policy on Discrimination and Discriminatory Harassment. The stated purpose of the code was to "identify and prohibit that speech that causes damage to individuals within the community" (*Doe v. University of Michigan*, 1989, p. 855). The critical portion of the code prohibited on campus:

Any behavior, verbal or physical, that stigmatizes or victimizes an individual on the basis of race, ethnicity, religion, sex, sexual orientation, creed, national origin, ancestry, age, marital status, handicap or Vietnam-era veteran status, and that

> a. Involves and express or implied threat to an individual's academic efforts, employment, participation in University sponsored extracurricular activities or personal safety; or

> b. Has the purpose or reasonably foreseeable effect of interfering with an individual's academic efforts, employment, participation in University-sponsored extracurricular activities or personal safety; or

> c. Creates an intimidating, hostile, or demeaning environment for educational pursuits, employment, or participation in University-sponsored extracurricular activities. (*Doe v. University of Michigan*, 1989, p. 856)

Anyone experienced in employment discrimination law will recognize this policy as a slight adaptation of the definition of sexual harassment under Title VII law. The policy, however, provided no insight into what was meant by such terms as *stigmatize, victimize,* or *interfering* (*Doe v. University of Michigan*, 1989).

A student sued anonymously, alleging that the code was a violation of his constitutional rights because it was so vague and overbroad as to potentially prohibit protected free speech (*Doe v. University of Michigan*, 1989).

In a swift and angry opinion, the federal district court judge agreed and permanently enjoined the enforcement of the university's new policy. The judge noted the absence of any evidence in the case that university officials "ever seriously attempted to reconcile the policy with the constitution" and deemed its legal arguments in defense of the policy "revisionist" (*Doe v. University of Michigan*, 1989, p. 868). Describing the university administration's interpretations and applications of various code provisions in the few cases that had arisen so far, the court concluded that the university was essentially making up the rules as it went along (*Doe v. University of Michigan*, 1989, p. 866).

Because the policy itself was constitutionally infirm due to its imprecision, it was not necessary for the court in that case to balance the relative interests of the parties, although it did express "sympathy" (Doe v. University of Michigan, 1989, p. 868) for the university's interest in providing and protecting equal opportunities. The judge also noted, however, that it was constitutionally unclear whether speech could be prohibited on campus solely on the basis that it offended another student (*Doe v. University of Michigan*, 1989, p. 868).

Regardless of the institutional or social value of the University of Michigan's mission to provide equal opportunities and to reduce racial hostilities on its campus, the policy in that case was clearly not written with sufficient regard for the protection of free speech. It may be tempting to blame poor legal drafting for the defeat, but the case demonstrates the difficulty any public institution faces when formulating and enforcing a campus speech code.

Meanwhile, the U.S. Supreme Court may have provided some additional support for hate speech codes in its recent affirmative action rulings. In *Grutter v. Bollinger* (2003), the Court upheld the University of Michigan's affirmative action admissions policy, declaring that "attaining a diverse student body is a compelling state interest" (p. 2327). The impact of this seemingly innocuous if not self-evident statement is potentially enormous. The existence of a counterbalancing compelling state interest is necessary to outweigh other civil rights, including the right to free speech. Thus, the civil rights of students are constitutionally inferior to the state's interest in establishing, promoting, and protecting campus diversity. The university in that case admitted that its affirmative action policy infringed upon the equal protection rights of white applicants, but because the court found the state's interest in promoting diversity to be compelling, the policy was upheld.

Yet to be seen, however, is whether the speech codes will be similarly found to serve a compelling state interest. Does the promotion of the state's compelling interest in diversity and equal opportunity necessarily require the suppression of otherwise protected free speech? Can a diverse and equal university exist in an atmosphere of hateful and offensive speech? Is freedom from insult a value of importance greater than freedom of speech? The courts will ultimately have to answer these questions before it can be said with certainty whether any campus speech code adequately protects, or ultimately violates, the students' right to free speech.

Many arguments in favor of campus speech codes draw support and analogies from the recent development of sexual and racial harassment law under Title VII of the Civil Rights Act of 1964. The analogy, however, does not necessarily hold. The learning environment is essentially and necessarily different from the work environment and should be expected to be more challenging than accommodating. Thus, the parallel between workplace harassment and campus harassment may lose legal support, giving weight to the freedom of speech and further curbing campus speech codes. On the other side of that coin, however, is the right of students to be free of such harassment. The case has yet to be made that a university's constitutional duty to allow offensive free speech negatively impacts its ability to promote and maintain cultural diversity. Institutions of higher education will remain in this difficult position until the courts draw the distinction between offensive language in the workplace and that in the context of higher education.

In any event, and as noted elsewhere in this volume, one of the emergent themes of the new student activism is opposition to racism, sexism, and other forms of discrimination and bigotry. This opposition must eventually conflict with the free speech rights of other students. Thus, at least in this respect, the constitutional battle on campus has shifted from one between students and administration to one among the students themselves.

One must wonder, though, what better forum exists for this conflict to be openly debated rather than prohibited by politically correct but ultimately restrictive speech codes. Jefferson's model of a free marketplace of ideas was designed not just for the protection of speech rights but also for the ultimate improvement and advancement of society through the public exposition and debate of opposing or offensive opinions. It is a widely accepted constitutional principle that free speech has at least as much potential for good as it has for bad. Is it not possible that otherwise protected student speech, no matter how potentially offensive or stereotypical or degrading to some other students, will have no greater adverse consequences on campus than it does in other public places? Is there some reason for us to doubt the ability of today's students of higher education to confront and withstand an offensive verbal assault? In this light, today's campus speech codes may be seen a disingenuous reversions to the model of university as parent.

Religion on Campus

The constitutional separation of church and state clearly prohibits any form of religious action or promotion by a state university, but the other side of the separation is the right of the students to freely exercise their religion in public places. Students must remain free to practice their religious beliefs on campus, and by virtue of the equal protection clause of the Fourteenth Amendment, are further protected from discrimination on account of their religious beliefs or practices. As noted earlier, it is now well-settled law that a public higher education is a benefit of the state, which is the basis for the many recent rulings confirming the rights of student religious organizations to use university facilities for religious activities on an equal basis with secular student groups.

Some institutions have found this principle difficult to implement. State executive and judicial officials are naturally leery of religious activity on state grounds or with state support, if for no other reason, then for concern about being accused of endorsing or promoting a particular religion or religious message. The recent dispute over the display of the Ten Commandments in the Alabama Supreme Court building was just one recent example of this ongoing tension. This concern for separation of church and state has been the defense espoused by some when sued for religious discrimination. And the courts, consistent with rulings in other contexts, typically have found the institution's interest in avoiding the promotion or advancement of religion to outweigh the free exercise rights of the students when the two conflict. To some degree, this is due to the reasonable opportunities off campus for the practice of religion without the necessity of state participation. But even accepting the relative importance of the establishment clause, the doctrine leaves at least two difficult issues.

One arises when students assert that the free exercise of their religion includes or even requires proselytizing on campus, the other when a student religious organization, which must be recognized and afforded benefits on equal basis with other student organizations, applies for funding that is provided to other student groups for activities involving communication. Religious activity that is also speech bears a double constitutional protection: the freedom to exercise religion and the freedom of speech. A case at the University of Virginia illustrates the problem (*Rosenberger v. University of Virginia*, 1995).

Students at the University of Virginia in 1990 published a newsletter called *Wide Awake—A Christian Perspective* and sought university reimbursement of publishing costs. Other student organizations were regularly provided such reimbursement out of a student fee fund. The stated purpose of the newsletter was to "facilitate discussion which fosters an atmosphere of sensitivity to and tolerance of Christian viewpoints" (*Rosenberger v. University of Virginia*, 1995, pp. 825-26). It consisted of articles about a wide array of personal, social, and religious issues, music reviews, and interviews with faculty.

The student group that published the newsletter had been recognized by the university and was apparently entitled to equal enjoyment of the benefit of the reimbursement of publishing costs, since they met all the requirements stated in the guidelines governing the reimbursements. Except that the guidelines themselves strictly prohibited any payment for publication of religious material. The university refused the reimbursement and defended its action on the basis of its constitutional obligation to avoid supporting a religious publication. The lower courts agreed and upheld the university's decision on the basis of the establishment clause.

But in 1995, the U.S. Supreme Court reversed the decision by a 5 to 4 vote, declaring the University's policy a violation of the students' rights—not to free exercise of religion—but to equal protection and free speech. It was admitted and obvious that the policy purposefully discriminated on the basis of the religious content of the publication itself and not the religious affiliations of its publishers. Because the university provided funding for publication of other student speech, the court held it could not deny the benefit to a group solely due to the religious content of the speech itself (*Rosenberger v. University of Virginia*, 1995).

The content-neutral payment of state funds for religious publication, decried by the minority justices as a constitutional first, was not, in the view of the majority, a violation of the establishment clause; it did not favor or espouse any particular religion or religious viewpoint because any religious group could likewise receive reimbursement for publication costs. The court was clear to point out, too, that no government money in the case went to the religious group itself for any other use—the payment was made directly to an independent printer. Thus, the concern for separation of church and state was insufficient to overcome the students' freedom of speech. The minority justices noted the apparent reality: Not all religious viewpoints will in fact receive state funds for publication under such a program because very few are organized into recognized student groups or large enough to produce such a publication.

Barely broached in the Rosenberger case was the next constitutional step: What happens when a student is deeply offended by the content of a religious publication that was published at state expense and objects to the use of his compulsory fees to fund it? A majority in *Rosenberger* apparently would support a challenge to the student fee on that basis, and Justice Souter predicted that the ruling, among other things, would make a "shambles out of student activity fees" (p. 899) in public institutions. Although *shambles* probably does not accurately reflect the situation at present, litigation under this theory is already well under way against several universities. The judges in those cases, at least so far, have rejected the challenges and sustained the use of student fee money for religious activities so long as the requirements and limitations placed on access to the fee money remains content-neutral (e.g., *Board of Regents v. Southworth*, 2000).

The Next Step

As the two cases summarized above illustrate, only the fundamental questions of civil rights in higher education have been satisfactorily resolved so far. Continuing litigation will not only resolve more marginal cases, but will also require judicial examination of the basic values of higher education and relative importance of student rights and administration authority. Having already won recognition of their basic constitutional rights on campus, today's students are left to the more difficult task of defending them.

References

Board of Regents of the University of Wisconsin System v. Southworth, 529 U.S. 217 (2000).

Cohen v. California, 403 U.S. 15 (1971).

Doe v. University of Michigan, 721 F.Supp. 852 (E.D. Mich. 1989).

Goldberg v. Regents of the University of California, 248 Cal. App. 2d 867 (1967).

Golding, M. P. (2000). *Free speech on campus.* Lanham, MD: Rowman & Littlefield.

Grutter v. Bolinger, 123 S. Ct. 2325 (2003).

Healy v. James, 408 U.S. 169 (1972).

Hentoff, N. (1992). *Free speech for me—But not for thee: How the American left and right relentlessly censor each other.* New York: Harper Collins.

Kaplin, W. A. & Lee, B. A. (1997). *A legal guide for student affairs professionals.* San Francisco: Jossey-Bass.

Keegan v. University of Delaware, 349 A.2d 14 (Del. 1975), *cert. denied,* 424 U.S. 934 (1976).

Kemerer, F. R. & Deutsch, K. L. (1979). *Constitutional rights and student life: Value conflict in law and education.* St. Paul, MN: West Publishing.

Millington, W. G. (1979). *The law and the college student: Justice in evolution.* St. Paul, MN: West Publishing.

O'Neil, R. M. (1997). *Free speech in the college community.* Bloomington, IN: Indiana University Press.

Rosenberger v. University of Virginia, 515 U.S. 819 (1995).

Silversten, M. (2000). What's next for Wayne Dick? The next phase of the debate over college hate speech codes. *Ohio State Law Journal, 61,* 1247.

Tinker v. Des Moines Independent School District, 393 U.S. 503 (1969).

Vaccaro, L. C. & Covert, J. T. (Eds.). (1969). *Student freedom in American higher education.* Columbia, NY: Teachers College Press.

Widmar v. Vincent, 454 U.S. 263 (1981).

Chapter 7

Working in the Wake of the Sexual Revolution

Holly Hippensteel

Campus Sexual Revolution?

Over 30 years ago, Robert Hassenger (1969) asked readers to consider whether American higher education was undergoing a campus sexual revolution. Evidence of the revolution seemed clear. Surveyed students spoke freely of their sexual experiences and the comparisons of seniors' responses to those of first year students implied that something inherent in the college experience was contributing to a "loosening" of sexual morals (pp. 125-145). Student fashions supported the sentiment that women were challenging traditional gender roles and becoming less reserved. The "mini skirt" was a clear example of women's new expression of freedom with their sexuality. Men, too, were challenging gender stereotypes by wearing more jewelry and letting their hair grow longer (Horowitz, 1987). Despite what seemed evident, Hassenger and some of his contemporaries questioned if what seemed to be a revolution was actually a phenomenon crafted by the media rather than a true shift in sexual mores. Hassenger (1969) worried that the media was making a mountain out of a mole hill , exaggerating the breadth of the changes by characterizing them as part of a sexual revolution. Though it seems clear that more was happening than just media frenzy, it is interesting to note the similarity between Hassenger's skepticism of the media and questions raised today.

Looking back, it is unclear what role the media played in crafting the changes that occurred, though it is clear that significant changes have taken place. Given the sharp contrast between what was considered acceptable behavior or conversation in the late 1960s versus what is acceptable today, one can confidently assert that a significant change in norms related to sex and sexuality has taken place. Of course, this cultural shift was not exclusive to college and university campuses, though the questioning inherent in an academic community, where discourse is encouraged, coupled with the tendency of adolescents to challenge the status quo, most likely expedited the change in culture on campuses (Horowitz, 1987).

But were these changes those of a sexual revolution? It could be argued that cultural changes related to sexuality came about suddenly and without warning, brought on by radical young people on college campuses. However, this explanation downplays the role that a multitude of societal factors, resulting from decades of cultural change, played in the process. Changes in beliefs and behaviors related to sex came about as part of the long term evolution of our culture, a development that was spurred on by societal shifts that supported and encouraged the sexual revolution of the '60s. For example, scientific advancements such as "the pill" gave women, and men, increased sexual freedom while also giving women more control over their bodies. The growing feminist movement supported women as they asserted themselves as "whole" people deserving of equal opportunities to express and develop themselves fully; it only follows that sexual expression would be a critical component of their development. The lowering of barriers for women accessing higher education and the increase in the number of women on campuses also led to a challenging of traditional roles for women. Lastly, the coming-of-age of the baby boomer generation meant that a significant percentage of the population were adolescents questioning the assumed morality of the generation that had come before them (Horowitz, 1987). All of these factors, and the combination of them, contributed to a climate that allowed for the sexual revolution. The sexual evolution of our culture, on campus and off, continued to be fueled throughout the 1970s and '80s by the widespread influences of Title IX, the Equal Rights Amendment, and the emergence of the AIDS epidemic.

In the 1960s students worked to break free of in loco parentis, establishing new expectations of student freedom and a dismantling of rules that regulated students' behavior outside the classroom (Astin, Astin, Bayer, & Bisconti, 1975). The Joint Statement on Rights and Freedoms of Students was widely adopted as the new standard for interaction between students and their institutions. The student rights outlined by the Joint Statement also implied a partnership between student and institution in the educational process (Mullendore & Bryan, 1992). The student was no longer seen as an obedient receiver of knowledge but rather as a contributing partner. While these newly asserted rights and freedoms had the potential to create more opportunities for dialogue and collaboration, the questioning of the establishment that took place led to a pitting of university and student against one another. This adversarial relationship between student and institution continued in to the '70s with students leery of the administration and even the faculty. Given the changing relationship dynamics between the institution and the student, the '70s and early '80s saw a "hands off" approach by the university when it came to the personal lives of students, especially their sexual lives (Horowitz, 1987).

Changes on Campus

Just as the post-WWII era brought on significant changes to the services routinely offered on campuses, so too has the sexual revolution. The shift in ideology related to individual sexual freedom, coupled with the demise of in loco parentis, has transformed many of the services provided by student affairs practitioners. Colleges and universities have attempted to stay contemporary in the services and out-of-classroom education provided to students, adjusting and expanding services to meet the changing needs of the changing population.

One area where changes in policy and practice are readily apparent is the residential experience. Student housing programs have moved away from single gender halls and curfews, even removing restrictions on overnight visitation by opposite-sex guests. Some campuses with coed living arrangements have begun to experiment with options such as coed bathroom facilities and room assignments. Many campuses offer options such as coed cooperative housing. Residence life professionals routinely outline expectations for staff members based on a holistic model of development that includes topics related to sexuality. Establishing boundaries with your partner, safer sex, forming healthy relationships, and ways to have fun without "going all the way" are all common topics for hall bulletin boards and educational programs.

The sexual health concerns of the 1980s also brought about shifts in the services provided by campus health centers and an increase in the role health care providers play in informing and educating students. As campus infirmaries have become health centers, most students can now access the benefits of full service health clinics that provide a range of reproductive health services including screening and treatment of sexually transmitted diseases, gynecological examinations, pregnancy testing, and dispensing prescription medication such as "the pill" and "the morning-after pill". In addition to the wide range of medical services now provided by campus health services, there has also been an increase in the role of proactive health education. Elaborate peer education programs and partnerships with orientation programs, residential staffs, and counseling services have come to be expected functions of today's campus health centers.

The AIDS crisis also brought about increased conversation related to homosexuality. As in the '70s, when women became fearful of feminism because of its links to lesbianism (Horowitz, 1987), the emergence of AIDS, once referred to as the "gay cancer", brought about a societal backlash against homosexuality. Though mostly negative, the conversations and debates sparked by the explosion of AIDS in the mainstream media opened the door for consideration of an alternative lifestyle and an acknowledgment of the existence of a gay community (Miller, 1995). The higher education community has since responded to this increased societal awareness with attempts to meet the needs of the growing gay community on campuses. Many campuses have expanded support services to include resource centers for lesbian, gay, bisexual, and transgender (LGBT) students, some staffed by full-time professionals who work to support, but also educate, the entire community (Vellala, 1988).

Together with these increased attempts to address the needs of diverse communities, many campuses continue to rely on the work of vibrant and active student organizations to provide support and promote awareness. The inclusion of LGBT students in the definitions and action planning related to campus diversity is slowly becoming the norm. The struggles for acceptance and inclusion of the gay community are not isolated to the campuses. The stage is currently set for the next battle on the freedom frontier as the nation debates whether all citizens will truly be afforded equal rights, including the right to marry.

Thirty years after Title IX guaranteed women, who now constitute the majority of students in college, equal access to education, we continue to work to create a supportive and unbiased campus culture for women. The hard work of the feminist movement in the 1970s pushed campuses to create women's resource centers and women's studies departments (Vellala, 1988). It also sparked an interest among women to pursue traditionally male-dominated fields such as the sciences and engineering (Horowitz, 1987). Though women continue to face gender bias, their access to and participation in the collegiate experience has flourished. In addition to the legislation that guarantees women equal access to education and educational resources, institutions today are expected to enforce well-developed and clearly articulated sexual harassment and sexual assault policies. These policies work to protect all members of the campus community by protecting the rights of students to a safe and respectful environment.

Role of the Practitioner

It is true that dramatic changes in acceptable behavior have taken place over the past 30 years. Social context suggests that these changes were not radical and sudden or revolutionary, but rather constituted a logical and natural evolution in the ways we think about sex and sexuality. Did the late '60s and early '70s mark a sexual revolution, or was it a turning point in the evolution that we, as a society, are constantly undergoing? Regardless of the answer to that question, it is clear that campuses have certainly evolved with the quantity and quality of sexually related services and information available to students. Students today come to campus having already considered their sexual options in detail, most having been exposed to some form of sexual education beginning in elementary school. What lessons remain to be taught by the time they reach the university? Given the sexual freedom, or at least freedom of sexual expression, that exists on our campuses, what is the responsibility of the practitioner?

First-year students who step on to our campuses have the ability to rattle off common sexually transmitted diseases; they know their options for birth control or "safer sex"; and they know that they have options when it comes to expressing their own sexuality. By the time students reach the campus, they are aware of the freedom that they have to express themselves sexually, but are they fully aware of the responsibilities that come with that freedom? It is crucial for practitioners to teach students the eternal truth that with freedom comes responsibility. Not only responsibility for the emotional and physical well-being of the individual, but also for the wellness of the communities in which we exist. Certainly, secondary education addresses the consequences of certain sexual choices such as pregnancy or contracting diseases, but talking only about potential negative consequences falls short of helping students consider the holistic set of outcomes related to their choices. It is the role of colleges and universities to assist students in identifying and considering these more complex outcomes of sexual decision making, going beyond exclusively physical aspects and concentrating more on the emotional and even spiritual elements of sex and sexuality. The role of the university has evolved from acting in the place of parents, to taking a more hands-off approach, to now aiding in the overall development of our students. The underlying message of much of our co-curricular educational efforts has become one of ethical and responsible decision making. While it is not an appropriate role to prescribe for students the "right" decision or the "right" way to feel, as may have been the tendency under in loco parentis, it is our role as student affairs professionals to pose thoughtful questions and engage students at a level beyond information sharing or surface knowledge acquisition. We do so with the hope that students critically consider their behavior, thought processes, and decisions from a broader context. As William Moore (1991) summarizes in characterizing the role of the student affairs professional, "In other words, student affairs is the organizational unit in the academic community that makes connections between the cocurricular and the curricular,...the cognitive and the affective realms, knowledge and action, and freedom and self control" (p. 768).

Unanswered Questions

The horizon seems to hold some interesting questions that will continue to prod us forward in the evolution of our attitudes concerning sexuality and gender identity. How far are we from the day when coed residence hall rooms, not just coed residence halls, are the norm? When will campuses begin large-scale conversations about the experience of transgender students?

Will women's centers and gay, lesbian, bisexual resource centers continue as viable means for addressing the needs of students and campuses in general? Will we continue to see a loosening of societal norms related to sex and sexuality, or will the pendulum swing back to a more reserved societal perspective on sexual behavior?

Exploration of this potential pendulum shift has already begun, as evidenced in a *Umagazine* article by Andrew Pulskamp (2003). Pulskamp's article, "Sexual Abstinence Hip on College Campuses", suggests that growing numbers of today's students have shifted their perspectives to a more conservative view than their recent predecessors. The validity of Pulskamp's observations, as well as the answer to the questions posed here, will come in time. While we wait to see what the future holds for our students, our institutions, and our society, student affairs professionals must continue to develop engaged and responsible citizens who understand that freedom of sexual expression does not mean freedom from sexual and social responsibility.

References

Astin, A. W., Astin, H. S., Bayer, A. E., & Bisconti, A. S. (1975). *The power of protest: A national study of student and faculty disruptions with implications for the future.* San Francisco: Jossey-Bass.

Bryan, W. A. (1992). Student Affairs. In W. A. Bryan & R. H. Mullendore (Eds.), *Rights, Freedoms, and Responsibilities of Students: New Directions for Student Services, No. 59.* San Francisco: Jossey-Bass.

Hassenger, R. (1969). A campus sexual revolution? In L. C. Vaccaro & J. T. Covert, (Eds.), *Student freedom in American higher education* (pp. 125-145). New York: Teachers College Press.

Horowitz, H. L. (1987). *Campus life: Undergraduate cultures from the end of the eighteenth century to the present.* Chicago: University of Chicago Press.

Miller, N. (1995). *Out of the past: Gay and lesbian history from 1869 to the present.* New York: Random House.

Moore, W. S. (1991). Issues facing student affairs professionals. In T.K. Miller & R.B. Winston (Eds.), *Administration and leadership in student affairs: Actualizing student development in higher education* (2nd ed.). Muncie, IN: Accelerated Development.

Mullendore, R. H. & Bryan, W. A. (1992). Rights, freedoms, and responsibilities: A continuing agenda. In W.A. Bryan & R.H. Mullendore (Eds.), *Rights, Freedoms, and Responsibilities of Students: New Directions for Student Services, No. 59*. San Francisco: Jossey-Bass.

Pulskamp, A. J. (2003). Sexual abstinence hip on college campuses. *Umagazine, November*. Retrieved November 13, 2003, from http://www.colleges.com/Umagazine/articles.taf?category= health&article=HN_000406sexabstinence

Rudolph, F. (1990). *The American college and university: A history*. Athens, GA: University of Georgia Press.

Stamatakos, L. C. (1991). Student affairs administrators as institutional leaders. In T.K. Miller & R.B. Winston (Eds.), *Administration and leadership in student affairs: Actualizing student development in higher education* (2nd ed.). Muncie, IN: Accelerated Development.

Vaccaro, L. C. & Covert, J. T. (Eds.). (1969). *Student freedom in American higher education*. Columbia, NY: Teachers College Press.

Vellala, T. (1988). *New voices: Student activism in the '80s and '90s*. Boston: South End Press.

Chapter 8

Freedom, But For What?

Rev. Christopher DeGiovine

Introduction

Dr. Martin Luther King, Jr. in his posthumously published book Where Do We Go from Here: Chaos or Community? (1967), said:

> We are now faced with the fact that tomorrow is today. We are confronted with the fierce urgency of *now*. In this unfolding conundrum of life and history there is such a thing as being too late. Procrastination is still the thief of time. Life often leaves us standing bare, naked and dejected with a lost opportunity. The "tide in the affairs of men" does not remain at the flood; it ebbs. We may cry out desperately for time to pause in her passage, but time is deaf to every plea and rushes on. Over the bleached bones and jumbled residues of numerous civilizations are written the pathetic words: "Too late." There is an invisible book of life that faithfully records our vigilance or our neglect. "The moving finger writes, and having writ moves on…" We still have a choice today: nonviolent coexistence or violent coannihilation. This may well be mankind's last chance to choose between chaos and community. (p. 191)

Dr. King had every reason to believe that the choice we faced then was between chaos and community. In our equally conflicted times we still are facing that choice and it looks like we are choosing chaos over community. Of course, Dr. King was speaking about our need to confront racism in the United States, but ask any reflective citizen today and you will hear a long list of reasons to fear chaos and bemoan the loss of community. Along with racism now can be included global environmental degradation, political and religious fanaticism, materialism, poverty on a scale never before imagined, terrorism, and on and on and on.

In the first incarnation of this book, Student Freedom in American Higher Education, (Vaccaro & Covert, 1969), a series of essays by various practitioners and academics grappled with the phenomenon of the revolution on campuses for more student voice in issues critical to the day. There was a demand for a greater voice in college administrative decision making on the part of students. American colleges had to learn how to deal with student strikes and riots over the Vietnam War, civil rights, poverty, and drugs. I was a student in those heady days and I can attest to the energy and passion that filled many of my fellow students as we honestly believed we were about changing the world. Perhaps we became intoxicated with our own false sense of power as we learned rather quickly that we could close down a college campus, get on the evening news, and continue to focus the nation's attention on our agenda. The solid foundations of the predominantly western European culture, religion, government (remember we thought we once lived in Camelot), and social order, upon which we stood solidly enough to rebel against the evils we saw in the '60s, began to weaken and crumble. The '60s revolutions had advanced the cause of student freedom, but now the question is, "Freedom for what?"

In his chapter on "Religious Commitment and Student Freedom on the Church-Related Campus," Sheridan P. McCabe, then director of the counseling center at the University of Notre Dame, spoke about the serious search among college students of the '60s for a deeper meaning for their lives. McCabe suggested that this search for meaning and the conflicts that this search created were rooted in the value orientations and religious commitments of the students of the '60s. He quoted Daniel Callahan who had written:

> Though there may be exceptions in every college, few students want to waste their time. They do not appreciate, and for very good reasons, having silly and wasteful requirements imposed upon them. They do not appreciate dull courses, poor teaching, dictatorial deans, petty professors. More than anything else, they value their dignity. If their university is any good at all, they will hear much about human freedom. They want to see some of it in their own lives. They will also hear much about the need for "maturity," "responsibility," "community," "service," and "personal

relationships." Again, they would like to see some of these values realized in their own lives. Not their lives after college, or in their lives at home on vacations, or their lives from two to four in the afternoon, but in everyday campus life, inside the classroom and outside, within the dormitory and off the campus. (Callahan, 1967, p.129).

These feelings have only increased in today's students. Students don't have time to waste on "dull courses, poor teaching, dictatorial deans, petty professors." So much is still the same. But perhaps a more interesting question is "why"? Why were students challenging the status quo in the '60s? And if students were rebelling in the '60s for the freedom to realize higher values of integrity and truth, are students still seeking the same today?

Callahan suggested that the students of the '60s would no longer tolerate these abuses because they had heard of and believed in the values of "maturity, responsibility, community, service, and personal relationships" (Callahan, 1967, p. 129). In other words, Callahan believed that student freedom in the '60s was for the development of the mature, responsible person who would be committed to serving her/his community and for developing healthy interpersonal relationships. If those outcomes of student freedom were true then (and I am not sure it was that clear and altruistic), it certainly seems more confusing today. Couldn't one as easily suggest that student freedom is demanded so immature behaviors can be continued unchallenged, responsibility can be shirked, the demands of others can be ignored, and a hedonistic "me-first" attitude can go unchecked? In other words, the quest for student freedom in the '60s may have been very enthusiastically, yet naively engaged because one can be free not only for the higher values that humankind professes but also free to engage our baser, more frightening nature as well.

McCabe continues in his essay to describe the challenge of this new student freedom to the more dogmatic, doctrinaire church-related colleges. He explores the tension between the free and creative intellect as it comes up against the systems and doctrines of established religion. McCabe challenges religiously affiliated colleges to rediscover faith in its basic nature as a search for meaning in one's own life. He goes on to challenge these institutions of higher learning to free themselves of repressive restrictions and allow for the free and unfettered exploration of ideas. Toward the end of his essay, McCabe raises the issue that continues to be at the center of the postmodern debate and is implied in the concern of Dr. Martin Luther King, Jr. with which this reflection began: the confrontation between the importance of the individual and the significance of the community. Although an increasing emphasis on the individual over the community does not necessarily create chaos, if the rights of the individual militate against the formation of responsible civic engagement and the development of healthy community, then chaos surely will not be far behind. Has the pendulum swung so far in the direction of individual freedom that we have lost our ability to form community? We academics like to think of ourselves in our respective colleges as a community of teachers and learners. We may be teachers and learners, but can we call ourselves a community in any sense except that which is most basic, i.e., a group of people caught in the same place at the same time? In other words, have we become free at the cost of the community? And if so, for what have we become free? Free at last perhaps, but now free to do what?

From the Modern to the Postmodern: New Concerns

The '60s freedom movement was an act of rebellion against a modern world that did not, and perhaps could not, live up to its promises, but its idealistic values cannot be assessed in a vacuum. In Roman Catholic theology God creates the world magnificently good AND there is evil in the world. Both sides of that paradox are true. Perhaps we were so enamored with the possibility that the newfound freedom of the '60s would allow us to recreate the world as magnificently good that we forgot that there is also evil in us and in our world.

The '60s were also a time of rebellion against a stable, ordered, modern perception of the world. At least in the United States of America, it was generally held that God was in God's kingdom, the Ten Commandments were the laws for living, our country had a manifest destiny for the good of all, and in due time science was going to solve all of the problems that plagued us. Ozzie and Harriet showed us how families lived. Life was, for the most part, portrayed and perceived to be very good. But all was not well in Camelot as we were soon to find out. The time was rapidly approaching when it would look like all that held the world together, all its central values and principles, were collapsing. Some like Kierkegaard, Marx, and Nietzsche saw this change happening long before others. In any case, the modern world was replaced by what is currently called the postmodern.

In the preface of their fine and thorough review of postmodernism entitled The Postmodern Turn (1997), Steven Best and Douglas Kellner described this transition:

> The postmodern turn is exciting and exhilarating in that it involves an encounter with experiences, ideas, and ways of life that contest accepted modes of thought and behavior and provide new ways of seeing, writing, and living. The postmodern turn leaves behind the safe and secure moorings of the habitual and established, and requires embarking on a voyage into novel realms of thought and experience. It involves engaging emergent forms of culture and everyday life, as well as confronting the advent of an expanding global economy and new social and political order. Indeed, the postmodern turn is global, encompassing by now almost the entire world, percolating from academic and avant-garde cultural circles to media culture and everyday life so as to become a defining, albeit highly contested, aspect of the present era. (p. ix)

Best and Kellner go on to describe how in so many areas of modernity something new is trying to be born. The '60s were a time of rebellion against what appeared to be a rock solid foundation of culture and experience that could withstand the seismic convulsions of that period. It could not. Perhaps the collapse of the Berlin wall not only symbolized the collapse of the great communist empire but was also a metaphor for all else that looked so solid in the world—cultures, religious institutions, economies, industrialism, science, art, and history itself. One can rebel with all one has against a power, a culture, or an institution when it looks impenetrable; however, once the foundations have collapsed, people begin a search for new solid ground upon which to feel safe and secure. In other words, the apparent unmovable solidity of the '50s allowed the student revolution for freedom of the '60s to occur. The uncertain postmodern time in which we live today is fueling the student search for a new solid, safe center.

Could this be the reason that small groups of students are reaching for new cultural, ethnic, or religious identities on our campuses? The major difference between the student search for freedom in the '60s and at the turn of the millennium is the foundation from which the search is begun. When a student rebels against a long standing set of values and beliefs, although he/she may want to change some of the beliefs he/she thinks are duplicitous, he/she stands on solid ground and can risk overreaching because there appears to be a cultural safety net that will hold in the end. But when a student lives in a time that seems to have no solid, or even stable, central set of values or beliefs, risking the high wire act of real freedom takes considerably more courage.

Two important experiences on our college campuses today reinforce the sense of multiple centers and various sets of values: ethnic and religious diversity. Our campuses are consciously and strategically becoming more multicultural and diverse in the student body, faculty, administration, and staff. Diverse cultures in different ways profess different values and hold different beliefs. Religiously affiliated colleges, and public colleges and universities as well, are becoming more and more aware of the need to respond to the inter-religious nature and hunger for spirituality of the community on campus. The 2004 UCLA Higher Education Research Institute's longitudinal study of student spirituality and how campuses across the country are responding to this need will provide a source of rich data to confirm this belief. Many colleges have already dedicated interfaith sacred spaces and provide opportunities for interfaith worship and spiritual growth on campus. Chapman University in California is currently building an interfaith chapel. This secular university has a heritage in the Christian community of the Disciples of Christ Church. In 1996, my own institution, The College of Saint Rose in Albany, New York, built an Interfaith Sanctuary with dedicated prayer rooms for Hindus, Jews, Buddhists, Christians, and Muslims, and a main worship space in which all the faiths can feel welcome. Endicott College, Indiana University, Johns Hopkins

University, the University of Kansas, among many others, have dedicated interfaith sacred spaces.

Different faith traditions celebrate different holy days with different rituals in different ways. Even though many of the core beliefs of the major religious traditions are the same, different religious traditions profess different beliefs and practice their faith in different ways. Our colleges now proudly report their growth in underrepresented populations and campuses are becoming more and more multicultural and inter-religious. While this diversity can add to the students' dilemma of finding a solid center from which to face the difficult experiences of life, and while this diversity sometimes can be the cause of tension and misunderstanding, in the long run this diversity is all for the good.

How do our colleges, especially religiously affiliated colleges, allow for cultural and religious diversity while holding onto a core set of values and traditions that will allow for the stability of its community? Are we all simply destined to become an amalgam of little communities? What will unify Hillel, the Newman Club, and the Muslim Student Organization into the college community? Will African-American, International, middle American, and Latino/a students see themselves all as belonging to one community of learners? This is the current challenge of the age of freedom that has been ushered in by the '60s revolution and the postmodern turn. In this time it is important for religiously affiliated institutions to rediscover, redefine, and perhaps transform their founding missions and clarify their central values in order to offer a new center from which the experience of teaching, learning, and developing can occur.

A Return to the Past or the Creation of Something New?

Students no longer enter a classroom believing that there is some body of unalterable truth which they must encounter and appropriate. Students enter today's classroom with their own ideas, feelings, and perceptions, which they believe are as valid as any other. Since all perspectives are equally valid, there is no need to challenge or engage another perspective to find the "truth". All truth is believed to be relative; it is simply one opinion versus another. If we are in a world making this postmodern turn to a new age, all that was once unquestioned certainty is open to question. Fair enough. But until our postmodern communities find their new centers, core beliefs, and values upon which they can agree and adhere, how does one negotiate one's way through life?

Public universities must become less frightened of exploring the rich and diverse spiritual heritages found in the great world religions. Religiously affiliated colleges can and must discover and reform their historical centers and add their voices to the postmodern debate. Currently these colleges seem to be opting for one of two approaches to the confusion of our time. Some are trying to recreate the world before the postmodern turn. These institutions see the world on a collision course with chaos. They believe that the only salvation for their college community and for the world is to reject the current freedom as libertine and destructive and return to those days that looked more secure. I believe that this approach is doomed to failure. Those days are gone and something new is trying to be born.

I believe in the other approach: Religiously affiliated colleges must recognize that the student freedom won in the '60s has as much potential for building healthy, mature, responsible communities as it has for destroying them. Religiously affiliated colleges have clear values upon which they were founded. These core values need to be rediscovered, reformulated, and broadly shared in our multicultural, interfaith communities. These reclaimed and reinterpreted core values and missions can form the centers around which community can reform. Chaos need not be the final word.

Public universities by their very nature need to be less cautious of openly exploring the religious and spiritual diversity of the world. What better place to dispassionately examine religious and spiritual diversity than on a public campus dedicated to the exploration of all the great ideas and traditions of the human spirit? Will our secular, public universities find the courage and the will to explore these important questions and offer multiple opportunities for religious and spiritual experiences? Or will a rigid and unclear formulation of the doctrine of the separation of church and state continue to paralyze our public colleges and universities and thus prevent this exploration?

Religiously affiliated institutions have an exciting challenge ahead. As we more and more see the tendency in our world toward multiple centers, increased intolerance, and prejudice, and fear of the "other," we hear the Dr. Martin Luther King's challenge to reform our communities and to refuse to choose chaos. This is the time to reengage the dialogue about freedom and responsibility; about caring for the needs of others, especially the poor; and about the need to sacrifice some personal freedom for the development and the good of the larger community. This is the time for open and honest dialogue between the cultures and the religions. Our campuses must more and more realize and foster the great diversity within our walls. The student revolution of the '60s for freedom for the individual is now meeting the question of responsibility for the common good and the survival of the community. The college campus, and perhaps especially the religiously affiliated one, needs to be the locus for these important discussions.

As the world takes this postmodern turn, perhaps all we can expect, certainly what we can request, is that we all try to engage these discussions with open minds and hearts. As we search for a set of core values and beliefs that will hold our culturally and religiously diverse communities together, we need to remember that the choice is still the one that the Dr. Martin Luther King, Jr. saw in 1967: chaos or community. The time and the task are no less significant.

References

Association of Catholic Colleges and Universities. (2000). *Current Issues in Catholic Higher Education, 20*(2).

Best, S. & Kellner, D. (1997). *The postmodern turn.* New York: Guilford Press.

Callahan, D. (1967). Student freedom. In E. Manier & J. W. Houck (Eds.), *Academic freedom and the Catholic university.* Notre Dame, IN: Fides Publishers.

Callahan, S. (1986). Conscience reconsidered. *America, 155*(November 1), 251-53.

Fides et ratio. (1998). Vatican City: Libreria Editrice Vaticana.

John Paul II (Karol Woytyla). (1993). *Veritatis splendor*. Vatican City: Libreria Editrice Vaticana.

King, M. L. (1967). *Where do we go from here? Chaos or community?* New York: Harper & Row.

Kung, H. (1988). *Theology for the third millennium, an ecumenical view*. New York: Doubleday.

McCabe, S. P. (1969). Religious commitment and student freedom on the church-related campus. In L. S. Vaccaro and J. T. Covert, (Eds.), *Student freedom in American higher education* (pp. 115-123). Columbia, NY: Teachers College Press.

Smith, H. (1982). *Beyond the post modern mind*. New York: Crossroad.

Vaccaro, L. C. & Covert, J. T. (Eds.). (1969). *Student freedom in American higher education*. Columbia, NY: Teachers College Press.

Chapter 9

Student Financial Freedom

Kevin Kucera

Students of higher education during the last 3 decades have experienced unprecedented access to American colleges and universities. During this same time period, there have been many hotly contested debates surrounding college costs and financial access to higher education. Since the original publication of *Student Freedom in American Higher Education* in 1969 (Vaccaro & Covert), colleges have had to grapple with extremely important topics surrounding access to education. Access and diversity have been intertwined within the ivory towers of higher education. No longer is the discussion simply about entrance requirements and how many students will comprise the freshmen class. Today the questions are much more complex, and diversity within the student population has taken a whole new meaning compared to the late1960s. Today, questions arise regarding the class composition in terms of the numbers of minorities, athletes, first-generation students, top academic students, women, wealthy, poor, middle class, international students, and disabled students.

The National Center for Educational Statistics (1995) notes that in the 1960s approximately 45% of high school graduates enrolled in college, and by 1994, that figure had risen to 62%. Clearly, access to colleges and universities has grown considerably over more than 3 decades, but the growth in access has been accompanied by increased cost. The College Board (2004) has noted that the average tuition and fee charges at private 4-year colleges in 1976-77 was $2,534. For the 2003-2004 year, that figure was $18,950. At state 4-year colleges, the average tuition and fee charges in 1976-77 were $617, compared to $4,694 in 2003-2004. Despite these cost increases, the number of students attending college has continued to increase.

Several significant trends have affected the affordability of higher education. Such trends include the shift of awarding financial aid based just on need to awarding it based on both need and merit combined. A second trend involves increasing reliance on student loans, coupled with a fundamental shift of student financial assistance programs to be heavily loan-driven. Another trend involves the use of technology to better assist students through the financial-aid application and award process. The economic climate and competitive forces among colleges has dramatically shifted the thought processes on how to attract and retain students. Overall, these forces have benefited students by improving their access to higher education.

In many college and university classrooms, students enroll in basic economics classes. At some point these classes will emphasize the advantage of competition in an economic system. Capitalism and competition are linked to create an economic system that is the envy of the modern world. Ironically, it is that same concept of competition that has made possible the unprecedented growth in enrollment across college and university campuses over the last 35 years. Competition has been a key to student financial freedom.

The first signs of competition working to the advantage of the student can be traced to the introduction of merit-based financial-aid awards, and the resultant shift of financial-aid dollars from need-based assistance to a combination of need- and merit-based assistance. During the late 1970s, colleges and universities were starting to experiment with these merit awards, and during the next 10 years, merit awards became a significant factor in distribution of financial aid at private colleges and many state universities.

What caused the shift to merit-based awards? Discounting for the purpose of this discussion the political implications and effects, market forces alone have encouraged or even forced colleges to become competitive in student recruiting. The pool for traditional-aged high school students was beginning to decline in many states during this time period. With the precious pool of potential college freshmen dwindling, enrollment management officers were faced with the task of offering financial incentives, often in the form of merit scholarships, to attract top students. Merit-based awards were also used to attract a diverse population of students who would not have qualified for other scholarships. What debate surrounded the implementation of merit-based scholarship awards has quieted considerably (see, e.g., Heller & Nelson, 1999), and it appears that merit awarding is now a fixture, providing students unprecedented access to higher education.

It has also become quite fashionable in higher education to promote an institution's racial, economic, geographic, academic, athletic, and extracurricular diversity to attract more students. Diversity has become the mantra for many college campuses. Obsession with diversity has created some substantial other financial-aid incentives for enrollment. The students clearly benefit from the college and university commitment to diversity, and from the fiercely competitive environment.

Competition for the shrinking population of traditional-aged students helped fuel the merit-based financial aid frenzy of the 1980s, but the traditional-aged student was not the only market experiencing volatility. The returning adult population has become a highly competitive market, and helped to keep tuition dollars flowing. To offset the decline of college-bound high school students, the working adult became the next target for access to higher education. Financial freedom was a major element in encouraging the working adult to return to school. Was this financial freedom sparked by the concept of merit-driven financial aid, as was the case with the traditional high school student? Actually, this was a different form of financial freedom driven by enhancement of curricular offerings and class schedules.

In order to attract the working adult student, colleges and universities had to create a delivery system that would work for this segment of the market. The working adult student often brings corporate tuition reimbursement dollars to the college campus, which in turn creates a new level of financial freedom, as well as access to education, for this population. In order to fuel the growth of this segment, many colleges created accelerated academic programs. For a working adult to maintain a full-time job and complete a degree in a reasonable time would be impossible taking one or two courses a semester. But offered two courses per 8-week cycle, the student could complete a full semester load in the traditional 16-week semester. Is the integrity of the course work identical when it is condensed from 16 weeks to 8 weeks? That question makes for compelling debate, but without a doubt the focus on recruitment of nontraditional adult learners has changed the financial structure of higher education.

In addition to creating accelerated programs in recent decades, colleges also have become enamored with the concept of utilizing community colleges as partners in higher education. Community colleges have been willing partners in this new alliance of educational communities. Community colleges were once the stopping point for students with poor high school records: Prove yourself academically at the community college and you will get the chance to gain admission to the 4-year school. A transformation took place when the community colleges offered more liberal arts general education requirements and eventually the associate's degree. As the curriculum improved and expanded, the community colleges siphoned off prime candidates for the 4-year school. Of course, the tuition charges at community colleges are a fraction of the cost of private and state-supported 4-year colleges. Thus, students have gained unprecedented financial freedom through these competitive forces.

Probably the single greatest factor in the advancement of student financial freedom has been advances in technology. Today, students can file a federal-aid application online, reducing the turnaround time and enabling aid to be received more rapidly. The real advantage to technology, though, is in the financial-aid office. The ability of the aid office staff to link directly to the Department of Education database has been an enormous help to all students, whether they applied electronically or by traditional paper copy. Corrections to the original aid application can be easily processed with immediate outcomes. Twenty-five years ago, a correction could take an additional 3 to 4 weeks to be resubmitted and recalculated. Today, the financial-aid office will receive immediate feedback from the Department of Education database to determine if the aid applicant has defaulted on a student loan, or not fulfilled citizenship or selective service requirements. Twenty five years ago, these were painstaking processes that impeded the aid office and dramatically increased the processing turnaround time, often resulting in students having to delay their enrollment.

Technological advances have also enabled students to rapidly and effectively locate more available sources of private scholarship dollars. Wonderful websites have been developed that offer access to databases of private scholarship dollars. These reputable services do not charge a fee for access to information. The databases make students aware of sources and application processes to enable the awarding of the private scholarship dollars.

Another advantage of technology has been the improvement of processing student loans. Clearly there has been a dramatic increase in the amount of student loans needed to enable a student to attend college. Much has been written about tuition charges that have exceeded inflation increases, while federal and state grants have not kept pace with the rise in tuition rates and the cost of an education. However, the combination of institutional grants along with federal and state grants, and student loan programs has fueled the unprecedented growth in higher education over the last 3 decades.

Students also have many more choices of excellent loan tools to allow for the financial freedom to attend a college or university when financial aid is insufficient. Federal student loan programs, such as the Stafford, Perkins and Parent Loan programs, have opened the doors of higher education to many students who would not have otherwise had the opportunity. Many creative alternative-loan programs have been created by private lenders, increasing competition in the market. In addition, creative new repayment options enable students to manage debt loan limits more effectively. While some are critical of the recent imbalance between loan and grant dollars in American higher education, there is no doubt that student loan dollars have afforded the opportunity for many individuals to attend college.

In summary, the multitude of changes that have taken place in higher education, especially the monumental shift of student financial-aid programs in recent years, have increased student freedom in terms of both choice and access. Some of these changes grew out of the lengthy debates that followed the campus upheavals 30 years ago. Debates continue over the perceived and actual benefits of student financial programs, but few would assert that students today have less financial freedom than their predecessors. Let us hope that, given more time and continual pressure, the trend toward freedom of choice and access will continue, to the benefit of both higher education as an institution and the student population it serves.

References

Heller, D. & Nelson, L. (1999). Institutional need-based and non-need grants; Trends and differences among college and university sectors. *Journal of Student Financial Aid, 29*(3), 7-24.

National Center for Educational Statistics. (1995). *Digest of education statistics and figures 1995*. Table 178. College enrollment rates of high school graduates by gender: 1960 to 1994. Retrieved January 5, 2005, from http://nces.ed.gov/programs/digest/d95/dtab178.asp

The College Board. (2004). *Trends in college pricing 2004* (p. 8). Table 4a. Average published tuition & fee charges, 1976-77 to 2004-2005. Retrieved January 5, 2005, from http://www.collegeboard.com/prod_downloads/press/cost04/04126 4TrendsPricing2004_FINAL.pdf

Vaccaro, L. C. & Covert, J. T. (Eds.). (1969). *Student freedom in American higher education*. Columbia, NY: Teachers College Press.

Chapter 10

The Impact of Educational Innovation on Student Freedom: The Case of Distance Education in Higher Education

Lenoar Foster

Advances in information technology have created new possibilities for innovative and flexible learning across the boundaries of time and place. Bates and Poole (2003) observe that "Web sites provide instant access to data from active volcanoes, Web cameras record events as they happen, and Web databases provide access to a multitude of academic resources" (p. 8). These advances in information technology are also creating new forms of electronic and interactive education—and freedoms—that allow people to learn anything from anywhere at anytime, thus creating opportunities for lifelong learning (Heinich, Molenda, Russell, & Smaldino, 1999).

The new technologies of the information age are changing both the nature and scope of interactions among and between faculty and students in colleges and universities throughout the country. Indeed, these new technologies have freed faculty and students to make more substantive use of their time and energies in shorter and more concentrated periods of time and space. For example, students and faculty may find that their time is more productive and better spent when communication is facilitated through electronic mail (e-mail), bulletin boards, or listservs. E-mail easily and quickly facilitates individual communication between a professor and student, or among students within a course; bulletin boards allow for announcements and directions to be delivered to all students in the class; and online discussions through listservs make it possible for all students to share ideas among themselves and to engage in discussion and debate with their professors and with other students. Videoconferencing offers real-time direct access to faculty expertise in over-subscribed courses on campus and to students who are dispersed in wider geographical settings. Computer environments created through the use of varied multimedia or CD-ROM/DVD technology engage students in state-of-the-art problem solving and decision making that are important to professional and personal success in an information-rich and demanding society. The use of the World Wide Web allows students to access faculty lecture notes and course information at any time and place, and use of the Internet provides an accessible resource by which faculty can link students to other websites from throughout the world to enhance, enrich, enlighten, and advance instruction and knowledge. Bates (2000) astutely notes that:

> Technology is used to supplement a somewhat reduced face-to-face teaching load, with significant elements of the learning conducted through the technology by learners working on their own (or in small groups around the same computer). At the other end of the continuum, learners study completely off campus (distance learning). (pp. 26-27)

Kearsley, Lynch, & Wizer (1995) have observed that "online learning activities are becoming a common component of higher education. While such activities began as a supplemental form of interaction, they have become a central aspect of many graduate courses and even entire degree programs" (p. 37). Arthur Levine, president of Teachers College at Columbia University, underscored the greater necessity and utility of distance education initiatives in higher education when he noted:

> Typical college students—18- to 22-years-old, living in dorms, studying full-time—make up only 16% of enrollments today. They're far outnumbered by the 19% of adults who lack diplomas. Many of these folks have kids, work irregular hours, or travel, which makes night school impossible. The result: millions of adults are dialing for diplomas. Study any time! College has never been more convenient. (Levin quoted in McGinn, 2000, p. 56)

The New Students and the New Demands: Freedom and Growth

Contemporary demographic and situational factors have coalesced to create a new kind of student in American higher education, one who needs and desires a new educational freedom. Interestingly enough, this new student is a product of the very society that demands that learning keeps pace with the rapid rate of change inherent in the contemporary information market and economy, and remains meaningful and relevant to the individual quest for self-actualization. Of necessity, these demands require new educational infrastructures that are responsive to flexible learning environments, schedules and delivery systems—something quite different from "the traditional model of college and university education throughout the world, primarily serving a campus of full- and part-time students and oriented toward residential activities of teaching, coursework, and research" (Foster & Watson, 2003, p. 6). Importantly, the new educational infrastructures must be sensitive and responsive to a host of variables that characterize the diversity of contemporary students in higher education institutions today, and that affect the degree to which students can benefit from their freedom to learn at any time and any place. Variously, these factors have been identified as encompassing combinations of location, age, gender, ethnicity, disability, and roles in the home and professional environments of the workplace (Bates, 2000; Bates & Poole, 2003; Foster, 1996a, 1996b; Foster, Bower, & Watson, 2002; Foster &Watson, 2003; Haywood, 2002; O'Rourke, 2002; Paist, 1995; Thompson, 2002).

Researchers generally tend to be in agreement that a new-found freedom to commit to life-long learning for personal and professional development has been extended to older students who are returning to institutions of higher learning in large numbers and who may not have the luxury of attending classes on campuses due to factors of time and location. These students are generally between 25 and 35 years of age (Holmberg, 1995). Haywood (2002) has observed, "It is common for mature students, those either catching up or adding to their portfolio, to trade academic community for convenience in order to run learning, family life, and continued employment in parallel" (p. 43). However, "in many institutions the 'typical' distance learner is no longer place-bound. Increasingly, students in close geographical proximity to traditional educational institutions are choosing distance study, not because it is the only alternative, but rather it is the preferred alternative" (Thompson, 2002, p. 64). Thompson (2002) adds that "[m]ost studies of distance learners in North American higher education report that more women than men are enrolled in courses delivered at a distance" (p. 63). Increasingly, distance education provides convenient venues for these older and nontraditional students who may choose to learn in either synchronous (real time) or asynchronous (delayed or staggered) contexts, and provides a scale of time economy for traditional-age students who prefer the independence of study provided through technology-mediated learning, whether they be at a distance or right across campus (Foster et al., 2002). Thompson (2002) states there is anecdotal evidence suggesting "that distance is a particularly appealing way for students from disadvantaged socio-economic groups to enter higher education, for many of these students, courses and programs delivered at a distance are an accessible avenue for upward mobility" (p. 63). And for young and mature students whose physical constraints and educational needs require accommodation, distance education and the technology that support it has literally eliminated numerous barriers. While federal laws prohibit higher education institutions from requiring students to self identify as disabled, Paist (1995), for example, offered that "approximately 3% of in-state students enrolled in the University of Wisconsin-Extension Independent Study program have either visual, auditory, physical, or learning disabilities" (p. 63). This increase in service to disabled students is expected to rise enormously because of the versatility of communications technology (Bates, 2000; Foster et al., 2002; Thompson, 2002). Bates (2000) observes that:

> In practical terms, we are seeing the following developments: an increase in off-campus teaching, not just for "full" distance learners who cannot access the campus at all but also for many on-campus students who find it more convenient and cheaper to study at least partly from home or the workplace; substitution in part of "real" laboratory work by computer simulations; new kinds of courses, such as certificate and diploma programs for those already graduated but needing professional updating; customized courses for specific clients such as private sector organizations, and multiple uses of materials to serve different client groups, such as undergraduate students, lifelong learners, and employers; partnerships and consortia that share courses and materials to achieve economies of scale and the necessary investment to develop high-quality learning materials; and

increased competition, not only from other public institutions enlarging their reach beyond state or national boundaries but also from new private sector organizations, such as the University of Phoenix online programs, and corporate universities (pp. 28-29).

Synchronous environments allow for participation in coordinated course sessions where students can essentially be part of local, national, and international cohorts of other students who are studying and exploring similar knowledge. Of this environmental context, Palloff and Pratt (2002) note that "it can be a dynamic and challenging setting in which to meet and can be especially useful in facilitating brainstorming and whiteboard sessions (*Whiteboarding* is writing or drawing on a shared screen)" (p. 332). Asynchronous contexts provide the greatest flexibility to learners who must be concerned about time constraints that are determined by other involvements and responsibilities. Palloff and Pratt (2002) note that, "[i]n asynchronous meetings or seminars, members have the luxury of time. Postings can occur at the convenience of the participants, allowing them time to read, process, and respond" (p. 332).

Who Knows Best in an Information Vortex?

Technological advances have done more than improve access to education and knowledge. Gumport and Chun (1999) note that "[a]t the basic level, technology has affected the nature of knowledge itself. It shapes what counts as knowledge, how knowledge is produced, how people are involved in the production of knowledge, and how academic knowledge is valued" (p. 378). And, at this basic level, lie both the freedom and the dilemma for both students and higher education faculties in this era of computer-mediated and Internet-based learning. For the essential questions then become: (a) What is worthy of being learned authoritatively? (b) How is it learned and from whom? and (c) What context determines authentic or reliable knowledge?

Within the information vortex created and sustained by the preservation and construction of the latest facts, figures, and interpretations, some of which are constructed for other purposes and agendas, the authenticity, authority, and influence of knowledge are constantly called into question, and the proper place and influence of the giver, receptor, and interpreter of knowledge are never a static condition. Indeed, within the vortex of information created by various search engines, knowledge and its various sources are inherently embroiled in the tests of reliability and validity, waging the battle for whose contextual and experiential realities can be trusted when, where, and under what conditions. Traditional ways of knowing increasingly give way to the importance and expansiveness of the learner's context. That is, the experience and reality of the learner become integral components in the quest for relevance and meaning as sources of learning. Bates and Poole (2003) believe that "it is important for instructors to recognize that the Internet, combined with a constructivist approach to teaching, changes the balance of power between teachers and learners" (p. 248). In essence, professors don't hold the monopoly on what constitutes knowledge and what doesn't, and the balance of authority in the learning process becomes more equalized. Bates and Poole (2003) further note that "[u]sing the Internet for learning moves communication of learning from an authority figure informing those less powerful and informed, to a context where knowledge can be shared and reconstructed among equals" (p. 248). This reconstructed space for teaching and learning creates great freedom for students and faculty, but it is also filled with great danger, as the translation and transmission of information is filtered among students and faculty and other parties for whom reality may be different. The world that students and faculty must be prepared to deal with is filled with questions that will be continually forged and filtered throughout the intellectual process to validate the reality and trustworthiness of knowledge so easily constructed, contrived, and retrieved through the vortex of information that is the Internet. Bates and Poole (2003) propose that these questions must be: (1) To what extent can I trust the reliability or relevance of a fellow student's contribution to a discussion? (2) How do I know the web site I have accessed is reliable? and (3) Where did this information come from? (pp. 248-249). In such circumstances how can the learner be sure that the material submitted for assessments is original work? To even a greater extent, the identity of participants (students and faculty) become a focal point of contest in the constructed vortex of the Internet and World Wide Web. Unlike face-to-face encounters in the traditional classroom, care must be taken that the identities of both faculty and students in the constructed learning space resemble, in reality and truth, what actually exists in fact so that the proper interaction and exchanges, characteristic of the social nature of the learning process and often so personally revealing and reflective, can be trusted and made safe for all who venture into the space of discussion and learning. This reality represents freedom to explore truths and reality in multiple perspectives at any time and any place and to be a contributor to ways of knowing hitherto unknown, undiscovered, or authoritatively recognized; but it also can create spaces of vulnerability, unwanted intrusion, distrust, deceit, contrivance, thievery, hate, harassment, and untold fear and dread that we have experienced to some degree to date, of which the more deadly and lethal potential may yet lie ahead.

Student Freedoms and the New Responsibilities in the Online Environment

While providing almost limitless freedom for students to access information and to interact with others in both synchronous and asynchronous environments, information technology and its utilization as a means of extending educational opportunity and access through distance education present unique challenges for the very individuals who have the most to gain and lose from its use. In this online environment, Bates and Poole (2003) state:

> Students need to be protected from plagiarism, harassment, and lack of respect from other students (and sometimes from academic staff). They must feel confident that even in an online environment, their privacy will be respected and they can discuss freely and confidently without adverse consequences. (p. 223)

Constructivist scholars argue vehemently that colleges and universities that venture forth into online education must be on guard against promoting technologies with packaged information that are devoid of reality, reflection, interaction, and decision making (O'Rourke, 2002). Palloff and Pratt (2002) and Dreyfus (2002) warn of the isolation that is possible in online education even when a connection without context is possible. They advise that "Textual communication is a great equalizer and can prompt us to be more thoughtful about what we say online" (p. 225). Others (Austin & Brown, 2002; Bates, 2000; Bates & Poole, 2003; Colyer, 2002; Dutton & Loader, 2002; Foster & Watson, 2003) argue for institutional policies that serve as criteria for participation in and contributions to online activities of all types. These policies are inclusive of attitudes and behaviors that stress the following principles: (a) academic honesty and integrity in the use of the World Wide Web and the Internet; (b) appropriate uses of computer facilities and online material; (c) ethical discussions about how relations on the Internet are formed, nurtured, and continued in friendly, collaborative, and productive environments; (d) respect for the privacy rights of others; and (e) the responsibility that each user of computer facilities and online resources must assume "for the material that he or she chooses to access, send, or display" (Bates & Poole, 2003, p. 224).

O'Rourke (2002) notes that "[o]ne of distance education's most significant contributions to the field of adult learning is its acknowledgement of the validity of the learner's context as a place to learn and as a source of learning" (p. 352). Information technology and online educational activities and resources that frame the delivery of distance education services to both traditional and nontraditional-age college students, many who may be residential or nonresidential, or both, on the nation's campuses, hold the potential to expand the learning context for all students. This expansion of the learning field represents an enormous opportunity for connections to the past, to the present, and to the future in the acquisition and dissemination of knowledge, as it presently exists and as it will emerge. What is abundantly clear, however, is that without sufficient safeguards and guidelines to frame etiquette and behavior online, and without the protocols (replete with consequences) that all can come to understand, internalize, and accept as important, no one will be free to realize his or her potential in the immense learning arena provided by communications technology to learn at any time and any place.

References

Austin, J. M. & Brown, L. D. (2002). Internet plagiarism: Developing strategies to curb student academic dishonesty. In L. Foster, B. L. Bower, & L. W. Watson (Eds.), *Distance education: Teaching and learning in higher education* (pp. 258-267). ASHE Reader Series. Boston: Pearson Custom Publishing.

Bates, A. W. (2000). *Managing technological change: Strategies for college and university leaders.* San Francisco: Jossey-Bass.

Bates, A. W., & Poole, G. (2003). *Effective teaching with technology in higher education: Foundations for success.* San Francisco: Jossey-Bass.

Colyer, A. (2002). Copyright law, the Internet, and distance education. In L. Foster, B.L. Bower, & L.W. Watson (Eds.), *Distance education: Teaching and learning in higher education* (pp. 88-97). ASHE Reader Series. Boston: Pearson Custom Publishing.

Dreyfus, H. L. (2002). Education on the Internet: Anonymity vs. commitment. In L. Foster, B.L. Bower, & L.W. Watson (Eds.), *Distance education: Teaching and learning in higher education* (pp. 71-79). ASHE Reader Series. Boston: Pearson Custom Publishing.

Dutton, W. H., & Loader, B. D. (Eds). (2002). *Digital academe: The new media and institution of higher learning.* New York: Routledge.

Foster, L. (1996, September). *University restructuring and distance education: A collaborative model for the delivery of a graduate degree program in education.* A paper presented at the 10th Annual National Distance Conference, University of Maine, Augusta.

Foster, L. (1996, November). *Graduate education and university restructuring: A collaborative model for degree delivery via distance education.* Keynote paper presented at the 14th International Conference of the International Council for Innovation in Higher Education. Vancouver, BC, Canada.

Foster, L., Bower, B. L., & Watson, L. W. (Eds.). (2002). *Distance education: Teaching and learning in higher education.* ASHE Reader Series. Boston: Pearson Custom Publishing.

Foster. L. & Watson, L. W. (2003, March). *The challenges of going global with e-learning: Infrastructure, policies, funding, and training.* A paper presented at the annual meeting of the Comparative and International Education Society, New Orleans, LA.

Gumport, P. J. & Chun, M. (1999). Technology and higher education: Opportunities and challenges for the new era. In PG. Altbach, R.O. Berdahl, & P.J. Gumport (Eds.), *American higher education in the twenty-first century: Social, political, and economic challenges* (pp. 378-395). ASHE Reader Series. Boston: Pearson Publishing.

Haywood, T. (2002). Defining moments: The tension between richness and reach. In W. H. Dutton & B. D. Loader (Eds.), *Digital academe: The new media and institutions of higher education and learning* (pp. 39-49). New York: Routledge.

Heinich, R., Molenda, M., Russell, J. D., & Smaldino, S. E. (1999). *Instructional media and technologies for learning.* Upper Saddle River, NJ: Prentice-Hall, Inc.

Holmberg, B. (1995). *Theory and practice of distance education.* New York: Routledge.

Kearsley, G., Lynch, W., & Wizer, D. (1995). The effectiveness and impact of online graduate learning in graduate education. *Educational Technology, 2*(3), 37-42.

McGinn, D. (2000, April 24). *College online. CXXXV*(17), 54-58.

O'Rourke, J. (2002). Canaries in the mine? Women's experiences and new learning technologies. In L. Foster, B.L. Bower, & L.W. Watson (Eds.), *Distance education: Teaching and learning in higher education* (pp. 349-356). ASHE Reader Series. Boston: Pearson Custom Publishing.

Paist, E. (1995). Serving students with disabilities in distance education programs. *American Journal of Distance Education, 9*(1), 61-70.

Palloff, R. M. & Pratt, K. (2002). What we know about electronic learning. In L. Foster, B. L. Bower, & L. W. Watson (Eds.), *Distance education: Teaching and learning in higher education* (pp. 224-231). ASHE Reader Series. Boston: Pearson Custom Publishing.

Thompson, M. M. (2002). Distance learners in higher education. In L. Foster, B. L. Bower, & L. W. Watson (Eds.), *Distance education: Teaching and learning in higher education* (pp. 62-70). ASHE Reader Series. Boston: Pearson Custom Publishing.

Chapter 11

The Political Involvement of Students

Aaron Kreider

Introduction

Student activism is alive today in the thousands of local groups working on every imaginable cause, as well as the student movements that the media features in its headlines. Since the '60s, student activism has gone through several changes, including an increase in the number of issues, a stronger commitment to antioppression, technological progress that has made communication easier, an increase in the number of national student organizations, and the rise of anarchism. Current student political activity is still influenced by some of the same issues that have been popular throughout history, and by an organizing style that often calls for radical change and the use of direct action. At any given moment in time, student activism is strongly influenced by the rise and fall of specific issues, such as the environment, sweatshops, globalization, and war. As this chapter focuses on the student activism in universities and colleges, it is important to note that high school students and non-student youth are also politically active—often in very different movements than those chosen by college students, who may be more economically privileged than their non-college peers.

Comparing Now to the '60s

When discussing student activism, typically pundits or journalists will claim to compare it to the '60s (CNN, 1999). Actually, they are comparing it to several years in the late '60s, perhaps 1967-1970, when it reached an unprecedented peak. If one were instead to use 1960 to 1966, or any other time period, the current level of student activism would compare favorably.

Ever since the recent WTO protests, journalists have been claiming that student activism is on the rise. For instance, in the March 29, 1999 *New York Times*, Steven Greenhouse wrote about the growing student anti-sweatshop movement as indicative of the "biggest surge in campus activism in nearly two decades" (Greenhouse, 1999). Unfortunately, no one has performed a study capable of proving this assertion. A safer assumption is that parts of the student movement have grown, while others have declined. For instance, it is reasonable to argue that the student anti-sweatshop movement was very strong in 1999 and 2000, and the antiwar movement grew rapidly from 2001 to 2003.

There also is little support for the belief that college students today are far more politically conservative than their predecessors. For example, a survey of incoming freshmen in the fall of 2003 indicated that they were more likely to hold liberal political views (27%) than conservative ones (22.7%). This has held true for the past 38 years of the UCLA Freshman Survey (Engle, 2004).

The unfavorable comparison to the '60s is often accompanied by the myth that today's generation of students is apathetic. Again, the evidence is lacking. Students may be less concerned about electoral politics, although recent activity supporting the Green Party in 2000 and the creation of 1133 campus Generation Dean chapters shows that many are still engaged (Kamenetz, 2004), but that is often because they prefer to express their views through protest and other extrainstitutional means which are harder to co-opt.

Antioppression and the Rise of New Social Movements

One of the reasons student activism appears less pronounced than during the '60s is that the emergence of new social movements has created a greater diversity of issues. While activists in the '60s focused on civil rights and the Vietnam War, there are now strong feminist, LGBT, Chicano/a, Asian, Native American, environmental, animal rights, and disabled movements to attract student attention. Thus, instead of students across the US focusing on strong centralized campaigns, there are thousands of local groups engaged in education or activism around local issues of their own choosing. For instance, Rhoads (1998) argued that the majority of student activism in the 1990s related to identity issues. Students of color, women, and LGBT students are engaged in struggles for changes in university programming, the creation of autonomous centers, new courses, and departments that would promote the inclusion of identity groups in the traditional university structure. They are active in combating racism, sexism, heterosexism, and classism on their campus. They are fighting for affirmative action, lower tuition, and increased financial aid. They are fighting for basic student rights, like the freedom of press and assembly: Pennsylvania State University students are campaigning for racial diversity, City University of New York (CUNY) students are fighting tuition increases, University of Notre Dame students are fighting for sexual orientation in the nondiscrimination clause, and Wesleyan University students want the right to chalk sidewalks. While groups on different campuses are undoubtedly working on similar issues, the lack of networking and communication between groups causes campaigns that might otherwise gain public and media attention to fall under the radar. Overwhelmingly, the majority of student activism is ignored by the media. This is especially true for the activism of less privileged students. Coverage outside of the campus media or the occasional local news story is scant.

Student activists today are united in their opposition to racism, sexism, heterosexism, and classism. Even if they belong to a single-issue network, they are still likely to address these additional issues at state, regional, and national conferences by offering antioppression training and holding caucuses. Under one commonly used system, caucuses provide a time for people of color, women, LGBT, and working-class people to meet in a safe space to discuss how they can end oppression within an organization, the student movement, or society as a whole. At the same time, the group of relatively privileged people (white, male straight, or middle- and upper-class students) meets to work on ending their participation in all forms of oppression and becoming allies. After meeting separately, generally both groups will come back together to share what they have discussed. The Student Environmental Action Coalition (SEAC), United States Student Association, United Students Against Sweatshops (USAS), and the Campus Greens are examples of groups with caucus systems.

Many students who are new to activism will question the need to discuss these issues, often arguing that racism, sexism, heterosexism, and classism no longer exist or that they are not personally responsible for them. It takes work to bring people to the realization that these issues of oppression are systemic.

Also discussing antioppression can get very personal. It can cause conflict as people become frustrated with the failure of student activist organizations to achieve their own antioppression goals. For instance, I have personally observed this frustration occur regularly at SEAC National Council meetings. A constant influx of students who are uneducated about these issues, combined with the continued existence of institutional racism, sexism, heterosexism, and classism, ensures that antioppression will always be an issue.

Unfortunately, antioppression is practiced least where it is needed most—at the local level. New activists are more interested in getting things done than in analyzing group processes and challenging the oppressive behaviors of their groups. Meanwhile, activists with more experience, who recognize the importance of antioppression, may be reluctant to rock the boat by bringing up these issues. In the short term, antioppression work can take away from the group's primary focus, and, due to high levels of student turnover, the short term is often the only one that matters.

The Impact of Technological Progress

Perhaps the area where student activism has gone through the most change is in the technology that students use in their daily work. How students participate in politics is shaped by the use of cell phones, cheaper long-distance rates, photocopiers, word processing, desktop publishing, databases, laser printers, e-mail, the World Wide Web, portable video cameras, and other technological advances. Young people are quicker to adopt innovations; college students have especially benefited from the Internet because it grew out of military and university computer networks. Technical advancements have increased students' ability to affect social change.

The technological revolution has made communication on a national and international level easier and faster. One can write an e-mail or post a news story to a website that will be read by activists around the world within minutes. The activist message has been enriched by including more graphics, audio, and even video, thus making for a stronger message than text alone can provide. Two downsides of these changes are a decline in face-to-face communication, and thus a depersonalization of activist ties, and information overload as more ideas and viewpoints compete for attention.

This increase in information availability enables student activists to choose how they learn about issues. Students can get information for free, without having to join any organization or pay any dues, so they are less interested in formally joining organizations. The most successful progressive student networks—like USAS, the Campus Greens in 2002, or the SEAC—will claim around a hundred groups. However, these groups have generally not paid any membership dues and are not all strongly tied to the network. National groups generally neglect to solicit dues-paying individual members, and most do not have any individual members.

Organizational Democracy

Contrary to what one might expect, advancements in technology have led to only minor improvements in organizational democracy. Conference calls and online Internet chats can and do open decision-making processes to a larger group of people, although no organization has achieved the mass level of participation which is technically possible by using e-mail or the World Wide Web. This may be because organizational process can be tedious, and many people feel that being involved in their local group is more effective. Currently, participatory democracy exists only for a small and often privileged group of experienced activists. Most national student organizations are run by a small, elected coordinating committee (Campus Antiwar Network, Campus Greens, Movement for Democracy and Education, SEAC, and USAS).

Organizational Diversity

Due to the increase in possible activist issues and the progress in communications that makes creating a network easier, there are now significantly more national student activist groups than in previous years. This contrasts sharply with the '60s when Students for a Democratic Society (SDS) and the SNCC were dominant. A lot of this growth has been recent. Over the past 10 years, only one major network has died—the Progressive Student Network (1994)—whereas seven new networks have formed: Free The Planet 1995, Student Peace Action Network 1995, Movement for Democracy and Education 1998, USAS 1998, Students Transforming and Resisting Corporations 1999, Campus Greens 2001, and the Campus

Antiwar Network 2001. Many of these groups are competing over the same constituency, thus decreasing the possibility of a united student movement emerging. For instance, the environmental movement includes the SEAC, Sierra Student Coalition, and Free The Planet. The antiwar movement is made up of the Student Peace Action Network, the National Youth and Student Peace Coalition and the Campus Antiwar Network. As most local groups have either weak or no ties to existing national networks, once every couple of years someone will push the idea to create a new national organization. The Internet makes it relatively easy to start an e-mail list, a website, and surf the World Wide Web to find contacts, which a new website, www.CampusActivism.org, makes even easier to do.

Leftist Ideology: Anarchism and Socialism

None of these new national organizations are explicitly tied to an old-left ideology, like socialism, social democracy, or communism. Thus, at first glance, it might appear that these ideologies have a decreasing influence on student activism.

Socialism and anarchism, however, have a large, subtle effect on student activists. Students who may not self-identify as a socialist, communist, or anarchist will often use these ideologies to support their arguments. They may not self-identify as anarchist or socialist, because these terms have a negative connotation and as they may care more about achieving activist goals than in getting people to follow a specific ideology. Similarly, most student activists will agree with slogans like "people before profits" and oppose "corporate power" before self-identifying as "anticapitalist." Ross (2000) found that students in USAS responded positively to socialism, and in a survey question about their political views 51% of USAS members chose the category that was furthest to the left—self-identifying as "left of liberal" (Kreider, 2002). Many student activists still believe that institutional reform is insufficient and that radical solutions are necessary.

Explicitly socialist organizations still play a large role on the left. For instance, the International Socialist Organization has been moderately active in USAS and recently very active in the Campus Antiwar Network. Similarly, the Young Communist League has been involved in the United

States Student Association. Whether or not student activists are directly involved in these groups, they are still likely to be exposed to socialist ideals at conferences and protests.

While socialism has historically had a strong influence on student activists, until recently anarchism was a relative unknown. Currently, anarchism has a subtle influence, shown in the emphasis on the importance of having an empowering process, such as the use of consensus, or near consensus, in decision making instead of majority voting. Ends are important, but means are, too. Displaying a healthy distrust for hierarchy and authoritarian leaders, the majority of the student-left does not believe in a singular path to revolution, or in the existence of a vanguard that should lead the people.

Anarchists are found everywhere, creating independent media centers, starting magazines and newspapers, running leftist bookstores, serving with Food Not Bombs, doing community or pirate radio, organizing critical-mass bike rides, staffing co-op stores, as well as forming official anarchist collectives. All of these activities expose young people to anarchist ideals. In addition, many people are introduced to anarchism through punk music. Since the World Trade Organization (WTO) protest in Seattle, anarchists have become famous for the confrontational activities of the Black Bloc, but this is only a fraction of anarchism's impact. The nonviolent, direct-action component of the large mobilizations against the WTO, International Monetary Fund and World Bank, Free Trade Area of the Americas, and the Democratic and Republican National Conventions of 2000 were also accomplished by use of anarchist methods of organization that involved autonomous affinity groups and democratic general meetings to discuss plans for cooperation. As young people influenced by anarchism join mainstream activist organizations, anarchism's impact upon the general left is likely to grow.

Similarities in Student Activism

In many ways, current student activism shares much with the '60s and the rest of the past 40 years. Some issues are always important, such as corporate power and corporate ties to universities. The latter was first significantly addressed by SDS, and currently is a main focus of the Movement for

Democracy and Education. Many national student groups are interested in issues and activities relating to corporate power. Issues often go through cycles of popularity; for instance, stopping CIA-recruitment on campus was popular in the '60s due to the war in Vietnam and also in the '80s due to conflicts in Central America (Mills, 1991). Likewise, student concerns about military-academic ties typically increase in times of war (Vietnam, Persian Gulf War, and the US invasion and occupation of Iraq).

Basic organizing strategy has not changed much. Students still educate people to gain support, mobilize their constituents to exert pressure and gain media attention, and escalate and use more confrontational tactics as necessary. The current mass mobilizations—Seattle anti-WTO, 1999; DC World Bank/IMF, 2000; Philadelphia Republican National Convention, 2000; Quebec Free Trade Area of the Americas, 2001—where police used tear gas and arrested young people are similar to those in the past, such as the 1967 Draft Week in Oakland, 1968 Chicago Democratic National Convention protest, and the DC May Day 1971 demonstration.

The struggle over who controls the student movement is still very important. Many well-funded, non-student activist organizations use glossy brochures, preexisting strategies, and numerous full-time, well-paid campus organizers to recruit students. Student-run organizations that exist completely independent of adult influence receive less funding and face tough competition for the attentions of local student groups. USAS struggles to remain independent of the unions which help fund it; the actions of SEAC groups are critical for the success of several of the Rainforest Action Network's campaigns; and the Young Democratic Socialists are directly responsible to their parent organization.

Major Student Movements

Within the past 15 years, it is possible to identify several issue trends in student activism. Student environmentalism grew strongly after the creation of the SEAC in 1988 and in the wake of the 20th anniversary of Earth Day in 1990. In the fall of 1989, SEAC's first national conference drew 1700 people and, over the next several years, students created hundreds of environmental groups. The student anti-sweatshop movement was very strong from 1999 to 2001 when it created the Worker Rights Consortium and, through the use of sit-ins and other tactics, persuaded over 70 universities to join. During this same period, students were very active in the mass-mobilizations against the WTO, IMF and World Bank, the Free Trade Area of the Americas, and the Democratic and Republican national conventions. The anti-sweatshop movement declined after achieving its major goals, and while it was transitioning to a general student-labor movement, the September 11, 2001 attacks caused student attention to shift. After September 11, almost all of the major student activist organizations united to form a coalition called the National Youth and Student Peace Coalition (NYSPC) to oppose U.S. attacks on Afghanistan and later Iraq, attacks on civil liberties, and ethnic, race, and religious discrimination. In addition, many students formed peace/antiwar coalitions at their universities which then combined to create the Campus Antiwar Network.

Conclusion

Student political involvement can and does change quickly. This is partially due to the high level of turnover in student activism. A group can easily lose half of its members each year. Often local groups will die after the people who started them graduate or move on. Turnover in leadership can be even greater as it often takes an activist 2 to 3 years before they become a local leader or active in networking with other groups. Thus, student networks are constantly changing, with national organizations dying and new ones being formed. Due to this turnover, as well as to changes within political, social, and economic conditions, it is difficult to predict what issue will have the most appeal to students several years from now. For example, there could be a massive campaign against the military's ties to universities, or the antiwar issue might disappear off the map. Regardless of whatever cause is popular at any given time, there will continue to be thousands of local student groups working on every issue imaginable, often transforming the lives of the young people so much that they will commit themselves to the lifelong fight for a better world.

References

CNN. (1999, December 2). *WTO protests awaken '60s-style activism.* Retrieved April 12, 2004, from http://www.cnn.com/1999/US/12/02/wto.protest.perspective/

Engle, S. (2004). *Political Interest on the rebound among the nation's freshman, UCLA survey reveals.* Retrieved April12, 2004, from http://www.gseis.ucla.edu/heri/03_press_release.pdf

Greenhouse, S. (1999, March 29). Activism surges at campuses nationwide, and labor is at issue. *The New York Times.* Retrieved January 17, 2005, from http://www.sweatshopwatch.org/swatch/headlines/1999/nyt_mar.html

Kamenetz, A. (March 16, 2004). "Deanie Babies" grow up. *The Nation.* Retrieved April 14, 2004, from http://www.thenation.com/doc.mhtml?i=20040329&s=kamenetz

Kreider, A. (2002). *Mobilizing supporters to sit-in: High-cost and high-risk activism in the student anti-sweatshop movement.* Unpublished masters thesis, University of Notre Dame.

Mills, A. C. (1991). *CIA off campus: Building the movement against agency recruitment and research.* Boston: South End Press.

Rhoads, R. A. (1998). *Freedom's web: Student activism in an age of cultural diversity.* Baltimore, MD: John Hopkins University Press.

Ross, R. J. (2000). *The new new left: From the sixties to the 21st century.* Unpublished draft paper for the PEWS/Political Sociology Mini Conference.

Student Activism Websites

http://www.CampusActivism.org: Interactive website that lists groups, people, events, resources, email lists, and more.

http://www.seac.org: The website of the SEAC.

Useful Resources

Loeb, P. R. (1994). *Generation at the crossroads*. New Brunswick, NJ: Rutgers University Press.

Sale, K. (1974). *SDS*. New York: Vintage Books.

Vellela, T. (1988). *New voices: Student political activism in the '80s and '90s*. Boston: South End Press.

Chapter 12

Student Activism Today

Seth Kujat

Note from the Editors: *The student unrest that marked the 1960s did not begin at Kent State University or at Jackson State University, but the tragic killings of students at both campuses in May of 1970 remain a poignant painful memory for student activists of that generation, as well as for faculty and administrators who were attempting to manage the student protests. Because the tradition and culture of both places still include those infamous episodes, student activism and the quest for student freedom may well have a different meaning for students of those universities. With that in mind, we invited a current student leader at Kent State University to share his insights and experiences.*

At every college, large and small, there lives in students the urgency to act. It is an urgency created by the realization that, as university students, they are legally granted the same rights as all adults. This urgency can evoke two responses. Some students choose to suppress this emotional urge and others choose to embrace it as a way of life. Those who embrace it are known as student activists. They create within themselves a power that, if used correctly, can change their lives and the lives of others. Those who act on this urge develop life-long experiences that will sharpen their vision, enhance their understanding, and increase their voices in times of complacency.

Student activism is still alive on the American college campus. Students across America today want to help change and correct the mistakes and wrongdoings currently taking place in society. This chapter will explain in detail my definition of student activism, including what makes student activism work and what personal techniques I have used to gain respect and the desired changes college students deserve.

As I entered college in 2000, I was unsure if I possessed the skills necessary to make meaningful changes. Quickly, I realized that one of the greatest aspects of student activism is its potential to teach students to communicate well and mold them into effective advocates for change. Fortunately, the molding process is flawed and activism becomes misdirected. The imperfections and poor assumptions inherent in this process are labeled by most as failures. But I would disagree because our student status allows us to place a "Proud to Fail" sign around our necks. This age of activism allows students to embrace their failures without worry. It happens to everyone (failure, that is), but those who learn from it will rise above it. College is all about failure and making mistakes. I have done it well and often for years and will continue to. But, I have learned that the best educators in college are the students themselves. As we learn from our college mistakes, we leave our campus with a greater understanding of the world and ourselves. This joyous process of failure helps prepare students for joyous times of success.

I have experienced numerous successful outcomes of student activism in my four years at Kent State University. One stands atop the list as both an achievement and an example of current student activism: the struggle to secure permanent funding for the May 4th, 1970 Commemoration at Kent State. This experience changed my thought process and perspective on activism forever. As an undergraduate student senator in September 2002, I was approached by a campus organization called the May 4th Task Force. They were seeking help to find funding for their annual event commemorating the tragic event when Ohio National Guardsmen opened fire on a crowd of unarmed Kent State students, killing four and wounding nine. This organization, and the event that created it, brought on an enormous amount of campus activism. I quickly researched the topic and found that permanent funding was needed to guarantee that this commemoration would always continue at Kent State University. I formed a support group, consisting mostly of other senators and May 4th Task Force members, and began developing ideas to fund the program. After much discussion and evaluation, I called for a referendum by the entire student body (over 19,000 students in 2002) to permanently allocate a percentage of a specific fee for the May 4th Commemoration.

The first step was to collect signatures from 8% of the undergraduate students, which began the first week back from winter break in January and was completed by the end of week 4. We did this in two ways: by petitioning in the main cafeterias, and by presenting and petitioning in the largest lecture halls on campus. I formed a small team of six to help with this task. After gaining legal approval of the wording on the petition from university council, we began presenting and collecting signatures. I made sure to remain positive and answer all questions honestly and specifically but found little in the way of strong opposition. On the third Tuesday of February, I presented to the undergraduate student senate slightly over 1,600 undergraduate student signatures. Then the problems and the excitement began.

Soon after, I received a letter from the University Council notifying me that the proposed means of funding the May 4th Commemoration appeared to violate previous United States Supreme Court decisions concerning the permissible uses of compulsory student fees, specifically *Board of Regents of the University of Wisconsin System v. Southworth et al.* (2000). It was suggested that I halt any further actions related to the referendum to prevent similar legal challenges by other students against Kent State University. I was shocked but also excited. Later that day, March 4, 2003, I encouraged the Undergraduate Student Senate to pass a resolution to approve the wording of the proposed referendum. Despite the discouraging words from our administration, the motion passed unanimously.

The following day, I received another letter, this time from the interim vice president for enrollment management and student affairs. It read, in part, as follows:

> It is the purpose of this letter to inform you that the proposed referendum regarding the distribution of student activity fees should not be included on the election ballot. This directive is based on the decision of the United States Supreme Court, and it is intended to ensure that the processes implemented by Kent State University for the allocation of student activity fees comply with the Court's decision. (C. E. Rickard, personal communication, March 5, 2003)

It concluded with these strong words:

> Please be advised that if the proposed referendum does appear
> on the election ballot, the results of the voting reflects a
> recommendation to me as Interim Vice President for the
> expenditure of student activity fees pursuant to policy and that
> I will not act on nor implement that recommendation, regardless
> of the outcome of the balloting. (C. E. Rickard, personal
> communication, March 5, 2003)

This letter was copied to the university president, vice president of
administration, chief university counsel, and the dean of students. Two days
later, on March 7, 2003, an emergency student senate meeting was held to
discuss the issue. I spoke out directly against the administration and urged
my fellow senators to band together and vote to keep the referendum on the
ballot. It passed unanimously.

Election day soon arrived, and after many long nights of distributing flyers
and meeting with organizations regarding the wording and logistics of the
proposed policy change, the referendum passed nearly 2 to 1. We could
continue our fight! I wish every administrator could have seen the smile on
my face. We spent the next two nights hidden away in the undergraduate
student senate office. Surrounded by law books, old court cases, and
numerous Internet law sites, we quietly formed our defense, and slowly
prepared ourselves for the unavoidable confrontation with the
administration.

I sent a letter to the dean of students telling him what our research
suggested, and that we had consulted legal counsel. Not an hour after
dropping the letter off, I received a phone call from the vice president's office.
They wanted to discuss the matter privately before any legal action was
taken against the university. I was thrilled both by the invitation and the fact
that our legal threats had worked. Things were working out according to
plan. We wanted to show them that, as students, we were not going to
surrender our voices to their fear of litigation.

One day prior to the meeting, I sent an e-mail to the vice president confirming our invitation. I also asked that he reply with the names and titles of those that would be present with him. He quickly responded: the vice president for enrollment management and student affairs, dean of student and student ombudsmen, the associate dean of students/director of campus life, associate counsel, assistant director of campus life, and one secretary. We had in attendance all eight undergraduate student senators, the executive director of undergraduate student senate, and one student secretary. We all sat down on Thursday, March 13, 2003, over 6 months after I was first approached by the May 4th Task Force.

I remember walking into the conference room barely believing that this issue had made it this far. I thought to myself that a lack of communication was probably the primary obstacle for both sides and I soon discovered that I was right. All the student senators were dressed in suits and each carried three ring binders with every point of our argument highlighted and supported. It was decided earlier that I and a fellow senator, Phil Eckenrode, would be the spokesmen for our side. We began by discussing the specific wording of the student-approved referendum, which university counsel had previously reviewed and approved. My fellow senator and I then stated our defense of the referendum. For almost an hour we reviewed specific points from three Supreme Court case rulings, proving that the form of funding approved by students at Kent State was perfectly legal, and, in one case, applauded by the courts. The administration representatives were all speechless. I am not sure if it was our well-prepared case or their poorly supported one that made them stare in disbelief, but nevertheless, they realized both the legal error in their actions and the determination and passion of the students involved in the cause.

Within weeks we finally reached an agreement resolving the matter. On April 15, 2003, the Undergraduate Student Senate, with the support of the administration, voted into policy permanent funding for the Annual May 4th Commemoration. The May 4th Task Force currently receives 1.75% of the annual student activity fee to fund the Annual May 4th Commemoration Ceremony (Kent State University, 2004). This guarantees that this historic tragedy will never be forgotten at Kent State University or around the world.

This process took just under seven months. There were three things that helped the students win this battle: (a) communication, (b) organization, and (c) motivation. Since that time, those same three things have helped me succeed within other student-related organizations and situations as well.

Students must remain open to communication. For an issue to be resolved or a change to be made, ears must be willing to listen and mouths must be prepared to discuss. A large majority of problems are created because people refuse or fail to communicate openly. Sharing your ideas with your opponent is a sign of courage and confidence, even though some will view it as a sign of stupidity and weakness. It is imperative that students do not become frustrated when sides refuse to communicate or barriers are put in their way. It is just as important to document all attempts and instances of communication.

A group that is organized has a far greater chance of accomplishing its goals. Everything must be documented and filed. It can be as simple as a folder of events or as complex as a computer program, but everything should be kept, including the group's and individuals' goals and strategies. This will ensure that new members will be working towards similar ends and will pass on the lessons of our experiences to those who will fight tomorrow's battle. It is also beneficial to read biographies of famous activists, such as Gandhi, Martin Luther King, John F. Kennedy, and Malcolm X, to learn their techniques and find out how they worked through their struggles.

The last thing needed is motivation. This is the driving force behind it all. If you want it bad enough, you will find a way to get it. Everything I have accomplished in college has been done with a strong conviction and never-ending motivation. Always find the positives and seek out positive people. If you are in a group that wants to change things on campus, my first suggestion is to get rid of all negativity, even though this may mean losing some members of the movement. They will only hold you back. Next, find ways to keep the group motivated. Often the simple fact that they are fighting the system or helping the community creates and maintains the motivation. If this is not the case, strong leadership is the next best answer. Find a leader that is well-respected and can motivate the group.

The many unsettled issues affecting college students today gives cause for excitement for the future. The challenge is not necessarily to win a battle or gain a reward, it is to find the passion to fight the battle and a cause worth fighting for.

I encourage students everywhere to find time to get involved. A large portion of my college education occurred not in classrooms, but rather in conference suites and organizational meetings. When opportunities arrive, reach out and grab them. I urge students to make college a time of personal control, a time to enjoy the freedoms from hierarchy, a time to enjoy the freedom from risk, and a time to grow emotionally, mentally, and spiritually. College is possibly the largest "learning bank" ever offered in a person's lifetime. At no other time are so many resources available to so many people at such little effort. We are brought into this world to do many things, one of which includes serving others. Students of the past, present, and future have done, are doing, and will continue to do just that.

References

Kent State University. (2004). *Guidelines and procedures for allocation and use of the undergraduate student activities tuition allocation.* Retrieved January 11, 2005, from http://www.uss.kent.edu/PDF/allocationGuidelines04-05.pdf

Board of Regents of the University of Wisconsin System v. Southworth, 529 U.S. 217 (2000).

Chapter 13

Student Governance and Leadership

Emily A. Langdon

"Liberty means responsibility"
(Shaw, 1903)

The last 30 years saw the demise of in loco parentis, the development of viable student governments, and a commitment to student leadership development, all of which dramatically expanded the purpose and scope of the cocurriculum in American higher education. This chapter explores how institutions approached student government and leadership development once they were no longer serving "in the place of parents."

Much of the student activism in the 1960s was in response to the restrictive campus policies guided by the in loco parentis philosophy (Astin, Astin, Bayer, & Bisconti, 1975). Consistent with that approach, institutions treated the frustrated students who were challenging the system more like children to be disciplined than like adults to be listened to and reasoned with, an approach that increased the fervor of the student unrest and, eventually, led to the downfall of the institution-as-parent philosophy. However, it also ushered in new opportunities for students to become more actively engaged with their institutions. It opened the doors for student affairs staff to serve as liaisons between the institution and the student, to ensure that development and learning opportunities were being provided for students in a variety of campus settings.

Through activism and legal intervention (Vellala, 1988), students gained both freedom over their personal lives and power in the form of influence on campuses. It was usually the student affairs professionals who negotiated and defined this new relationship between students and their institutions (Carpenter, 1991). Student affairs professionals' roles shifted from that of disciplinarian to more of an advisor, coordinator, and indeed, educator

(Garland, 1985; Garland & Grace, 1993). These staff members began to serve as student advocates on campus and replaced the controlling, disciplinarian approach with a philosophy that came to be known as student development.

Those institutions that understood, as George Bernard Shaw (1903) did, that "liberty means responsibility" began providing opportunities for students to assume more responsibility in the management of their educational environment. Resident assistant positions in residence halls and service on judicial boards empowered students to hold their peers accountable for inappropriate behavior. This was a powerful experience for both the student body at large and for the student in the role of paraprofessional (Ender & Carranza, 1991). Institutions successfully tapped into the most influential relationship on the college campus: the peer group (Astin, 1993).

On most campuses, students are now actively involved in some component of the student judicial process (Spitzberg & Thorndike, 1992). Although many institutions reserve the right for purely administrative hearings, student judicial boards often handle violations of academic integrity, such as plagiarism and cheating, usually in collaboration with faculty.

> The student disciplinary process can be one that allows the participating students to experience the exercise of citizenship in a setting where he or she serves others and also makes decisions that affect the lives of fellow students, sometimes significantly. (Spitzberg & Thorndike, 1992, p. 104)

Thus, meaningful, authentic student involvement in processes such as peer accountability can provide students with powerful lessons on citizenship and leadership.

Often students have even more autonomy over their own affairs in the campus life arena. In residence halls, in student organizations, and in student government, students have considerable responsibility for the expenditure of funds, the development of community spirit, and the creation of policies and procedures. Student government involvement can truly empower student leaders since administrators often serve more as advisors than supervisors, and student government officers often hold significant authority over the distribution of funds and decisions about student policies and organizations (Cuyjet, 1994). Thus, the student government is an incredible vehicle for empowering students, tapping into the power of peer relationships and providing opportunities to develop leadership capacities.

Evolution of Student Governance

As the nature of the relationship between the student and the institution changed, the power of the student and the role of the student government also shifted. Since legal battles decimated the doctrine of in loco parentis, students gained more autonomy over their personal lives and decision making, leading, in time, to increased influence of student governments.

Student governments began appearing on college campuses between 1900 and 1920 spurred by the Progressive period in the United States (Rudolph, 1962), but in their earlier years they were used as a tool of the administration to help control student behavior. Student governments were more likely to provide input on campus policies on a superficial level, with no decision making authority or influence regarding student life (Horowitz, 1987). Student radicals attempted to increase the power of the student government in the 1930s, but real change was not realized until the student unrest of the 1960s (Cohen, 1998). Cohen (1998) addresses the role of student governments in what he refers to as the University Transformation Era (1870-1944):

> The students in American institutions never developed the type of political power enjoyed by their counterparts in Europe and Latin America. Most institutions developed some form of student government, but only rarely did it grow past the stage of responsibility for extracurricular activities. (p. 157)

In 1967, the AAUP gathered together national associations representing various constituencies in higher education and crafted a Joint Statement of Rights and Freedoms of Students (Mullendore, 1992). This document outlined the need for individual students, as well as collective student organizations, to have input on institutional policies. Most student governments have constitutions that clarify the students' rights and responsibilities, often designating the academic and student life committees where students have representation (Bryan, 1992). The role of student governments expanded as student leaders began to make meaningful contributions to decisions about student life policies and academic procedures. Students' perspectives were gaining representation in university decisions as students were allowed to serve on student life committees, faculty committees, and even Board of Trustees committees (Klumpyan & Langdon, 2000; Nuss, 1996).

But what do student governments really do? According to a survey of over 200 colleges, student governments provide, in order of most frequent responses, representation on campus-wide committees, activities programming, allocation of student activities fee, recognition of student organizations, and participation in institutional governance (Cuyjet, 1994). Depending on the type of institution and campus culture, student governments have developed varying degrees of power and autonomy over campus matters. Some are responsible solely for co-curricular programming, while others are actively involved in serious decisions affecting both student life and academic processes. Involvement of student governments and student organizations falls along a continuum of power and participation from "party planners" to "policy makers". Cohen (1998) argued that the most influence was gained by students who formed statewide student associations and public interest research groups. These groups are able to lobby and to provide pressure that influences public decision makers.

Regardless of how much legitimate power students have in institutional decision making, fostering effective student involvement in governance signifies an institution's commitment to student leadership development (Schoenberg, 1992). Today's college student has access to more participation in institutional decision making, but many do not exercise these rights and privileges. For years, few students have voted in student government elections (Levine & Cureton, 1998; Mable & DeCoster, 1981), which is not surprising, given our country's record for voting in national elections, especially among the youngest voters.

If students are to effectively serve on faculty committees, advise institutional governing boards and presidents, hold responsibilities for student life functions such as members of judicial board and residence hall governing councils, lobby legislators and policymakers, distribute student activity fees, and provide entertainment and educational activities to the campus at large, institutions need to ensure that students have the skills, support systems, and authority required to carry out these responsibilities successfully. But students have gained more control over their own lives, as well as their own organizations, and they have taken an expanded role in institutional decision making, which has provided more student leadership opportunities while simultaneously revealing the desirability of meaningful student leadership training, education, and development (Roberts & Ullom, 1989).

Rise of the Leadership Development Movement

Many colleges and universities identify leadership as a goal of undergraduate education (Boyer, 1987; Schoenberg, 1992). Since the colonial period, higher education has assumed the role of preparing citizens to participate as leaders in a democratic society (Rudolph, 1962). Many institutions include in their mission statements the development of leaders for the survival of the republic (Miller & Jones, 1981). Boyer (1987) argued that students should not only be invited, but also should be expected to participate in campus decision making, because college is the time to develop a commitment to active citizenship, with the end result being good for both the individual and society. This is good for the future of not just the individual, but of democracy. As society grows more complex, higher education must help these future leaders manage the increasing complexity. One of the ways to do that is to help students create and cope with change (Roberts & Ullom, 1989; Kotter, 1996; Higher Education Research Institute, 1996).

Burns (1978) identified a national leadership crisis and started an on-going debate (Mangan, 2002) about the interdisciplinary field of leadership studies. Many colleges and universities provide leadership training for college students, often coordinated and delivered by the student affairs professionals who for some time now have argued that the purpose of their work is the development of the whole person (American Council on Education, 1937/1994). Most leadership programs are focused on skills development for practical purposes and applied in the realm of student government and student organizations. A more recent movement within the leadership field is the interdisciplinary field known as leadership studies, which has moved leadership toward the center of the student learning experience by including it in the curriculum (Mangan, 2002).

In *When Dreams and Heroes Died*, Levine (1980) suggested that the undergraduate experience would be more meaningful to students and more helpful to society if it included the treatment of values, addressed ethical questions, identified problems common to humanity, and offered creative ways for groups to solve them. Additionally, Astin (1993) demonstrated that increases in leadership skills are associated with the college experience, which should compel colleges and universities to take seriously the opportunities for leadership development that exist today on the campus. Higher education has the opportunity to create leaders, to train individuals to engage in the betterment of their communities, and foster the commitment to civic engagement needed to adequately address the complex problems facing our society and our world: in other words, to fulfill the promise of higher education in America.

Ensuring that student governments are, indeed, learning environments requires meaningful, genuine opportunities for students to lead. Thus, institutions need to share power, or empower all members of student leadership organizations. The research in higher education is clear: Astin (1993) found that being elected to student office was positively associated in a student's self-reported leadership abilities. The qualitative exploration of "involving colleges" (Kuh, Schuh, & Whitt, 1991) demonstrated that students at these committed institutions know how the place works. They take responsibility for their lives and their learning, and the institution provides ample opportunities for them to discover and develop their leadership capacities. "At all of the Involving Colleges, students play an active and substantial role in institutional governance" (Kuh et al., 1991, p. 325). These researchers found that these institutions trust students and hold high expectations for them. This finding was supported by campus artifacts, such as honor codes and residence life policies, and a commitment to promoting student initiatives.

Leadership is certainly about those with titles, but it is also about those who are active participants in groups and organizations, those who contribute without benefit of a formal title or role (Rost, 1991; Rogers, 1996; McMahon, 2001), suggesting that the collegiate student organizations are the optimal places to foster leadership development. One does not need to be the student government president to exercise leadership, to hone leadership skills, to initiate projects, and to create change (Bonous-Hammarth, 2001). Student organizations are ideal laboratories for students interested in learning leadership, especially how to apply leadership theory to the actual practice of being a leader (Roberts & Ullom, 1989). This is a compelling argument for students to explore, and for institutions to support, leadership as an intellectual enterprise, not just a cocurricular distraction (Langdon & Mathias, 2001).

One of the serious constraints that impede campus-wide student empowerment and leadership development, while simultaneously fostering student apathy, is the concentration of decision making authority among a handful of campus administrators. These administrators are often unwilling to share power or decision making with student leaders or student organizations (Downey, 1981). When institutions do not truly engage students, they negate the empowering potential of student government. Instead, "student governments have no real decision-making authority; lack continuity and cohesiveness; have no mentors or even committed advisors and advocates; have no formalized training" (Downey, 1981, p. 83).

Some campus administrators may ignore the opportunities for student involvement because of the commitment required of those responsible to implement it. A primer on effective training (Morrell & Morrell, 1986) promotes combinations of formal training, informal on-the-job training, and/or written contracts specifying the duties of each student officer. Even these basic training experiences take a commitment of time, financial resources, and substantial energy on behalf of the student affairs staff.

And yet, these introductory training sessions still do not address the power dynamics or structural issues that are necessary for students to influence change or have genuine access to decision making. If student affairs professionals seriously want student governments to succeed and student leaders to have meaningful experiences that come from having made lasting contributions, they need to provide sophisticated training and preparation in such matters as:

- "[A]nalyzing the power structure on campus and its relation to society; determining how to work with the power structure and make it more responsive; designing strategies to bring about desired change; [and] evaluating the effectiveness of their programs" (Downey, 1981, 83-84).

- Many student affairs professionals do not have the skills, time, or understanding to provide this level of training and mentoring. For those who do, the results can be both personally transformational as well as impactful across the campus (Klumpyan & Langdon, 2000).

- Student government must be meaningful to be credible. Token participation or involvement that is limited to peripheral, unimportant matters confirms the suspicion that students are not fully part of decision making, breeding disillusionment, distrust, and alienation (Mable & DeCoster, 1981). On the other hand, how can a student government be taken seriously by a campus administration when voter turnout is abysmal? Candidates run unopposed, offices are left empty until someone is finally appointed, meetings are fruitless as students vie for power, and there is rarely a functioning communication mechanism to gain the views and ideas of the students they represent (Mable & DeCoster, 1981).

To help make student governments work, colleges and universities should make the necessary investment to provide the things that the student organizations lack. Since college is a short 4- to 5-year endeavor, there will always be a turnover issue. Campus administrators can ensure that the student government is well-advised, facilitating continuity by assigning experienced staff members to the advisor roles. There needs to be a commitment to better training, and special attention paid to the transition between student administrations. Student affairs professionals need to see themselves as student advocates, to reinforce positive initiatives from the student government, and help pave the way for students to make certain that their concerns are heard.

A Look Ahead

What lies ahead is uncertain as each generation of students brings new challenges to the learning environment. The world is changing rapidly, yet institutions of higher education often seem unable or uninterested in keeping pace. One might argue that the pendulum is swinging back toward an in loco parentis attitude given that parents of the "millennial" generation (Howe & Strauss, 2000) are more involved in the lives of their children than was any previous generation of parents. This high level of parental involvement, coupled with an increasing litigious society, is pushing institutions to take more control over the collegiate environment in an effort to reduce exposure to risk and criticism. Some campus administrators interpret this as a call to return to the hands-on role once held by campus disciplinarians. A Harvard professor who offers advice on how to create positive, engaging learning environments (Light, 2001), suggests that institutions not "get out of the way" but indeed "get in the students' way" (pp. 209-210). The stories he relates are in the spirit of student empowerment and engagement, but there could be an interpretation harkening back to the days of parental control by campus administrators. Will our campuses regress? Will the freedoms gained by students be replaced by administrators more interested in risk management than in student learning?

Instead of moving backward in time, today's campus administrators and, in particular, student affairs administrators, will need to recommit themselves and their institutions to the education of the whole student, the holistic approach to education that was articulated in the student development movement. In the future, a new and expanded look at holistic education should take not only the student into consideration, but the entire campus, including the collegiate experience.

> [L]earning must be reconsidered...new research, changing
> times, and the needs of today's emerging generation of students
> require that our traditionally distinct categories of academic
> learning and student development be fused in an integrated,
> comprehensive vision of learning as a transformative process
> that is centered in and responsive to the whole student."
> (American College Personnel Association & National
> Association of Student Personnel Administrators, 2004, p. 30)

This approach reflects our more complex world as well as our increased access to technology and communication mechanisms. It isn't just about educating the students, it's about providing an engaging, educational environment.

Careful, thoughtful campus administrators will need to commit to an integrated approach to education. Institutions would do well to focus on three elements of the campus: people, process, and place (Performa, 2004). Colleges that engage students in their own learning and in the setting of institutional goals and the making of decisions are certainly focusing on the "people" component. One way this can be demonstrated is through an institutional commitment to student leadership development addressed earlier. Think how much time is dedicated to personnel issues on campus and consider that a significant portion of the higher education budget is allocated to salaries. Education is a relational, labor-intensive, people-oriented business. Thus, few campuses can afford not to focus on its people.

Institutions of higher education are also large bureaucracies, so an emphasis on process is important. A campus can decide which processes to invest in, to spend their limited time and money on. One example of a campus process frequently in need of attention might be the increasing dependence on technology and the growing gap of interest in and understanding of technology between students and their professors. Clearly, integrated campuses will focus not only on people and processes but also on the place where the student learning is to occur. These campuses will have the advantage of actively and purposefully engaging students in their own educations.

The focus on place often seems less important to student affairs professionals, who are often so people-oriented, and other campus administrators, whose jobs involve creating systems and processes. However, place is critical (Kirk, 1999). The campus environment sends messages to students everyday. Campuses, intentionally or not, tell students if their involvement is important or unimportant. An institutional assessment of the environment can help a campus determine what is being communicated to students and how (Strange & Banning, 2001) through its place, the physical plant. And, once again, student affairs professionals can lead the way in involving students in this process so that even a campus assessment is used as a learning opportunity, a leadership development experience, and a way to engage students in the meaningful work of the institution.

As an experienced senior student affairs administrator now serving as a campus planning consultant, I have become aware of the importance of integrating the elements of people, process and place, to ensure a holistic approach to decision making. The special role that student affairs professionals can play in institutional decision making is to pay attention to each of these three critical components. Student affairs staff members need to understand the power of involving people in decisions, to care about streamlining processes to serve (not frustrate) students, and, finally, to ensure that campus is comprised of places and spaces that embody powerful learning (Schroeder & Mable, 1994). If student affairs professionals believe in the holistic education of students and translate that to the entire campus environment, they can champion the concept of integrated campus planning, and convey to other campus decision makers the powerful impact of addressing people, process, and place in strategic decision making and planning.

References

American College Personnel Association & National Association of Student Personnel Administrators. (2004). *Learning reconsidered: A campus-wide focus on the student experience*. Washington, DC: Authors.

American Council on Education. (1994). The student personnel point of view. In A. L. Rentz (Ed.), *Student affairs: A profession's heritage.* Lanham, MD: University Press of America (Original work published in 1937).

Astin, A. W. (1993). *What matters in college: Four critical years revisited.* San Francisco: Jossey-Bass.

Astin, A. W., Astin, H. S., Bayer, A.E., & Bisconti, A. S. (1975). *The power of protest: A national study of student and faculty disruptions with implications for the future.* San Francisco: Jossey-Bass.

Bonous-Hammarth, M. (2001). Developing social change agents: Leadership development for the 1990s and beyond. In C.L. Outcalt, S. K.Ferris, & K. N. MacMahon (Eds.), *Developing nonhierarchical leadership on campus.* Westport, CT: Greenwood Press.

Boyer, E. L. (1987). *College: The undergraduate experience in America.* New York: Harper Collins.

Bryan, W. A. (1992). Student Affairs. In W. A. Bryan & R. H. Mullendore (Eds.), *Rights, Freedoms, and Responsibilities of Students: New Directions for Student Services, No. 59.* San Francisco: Jossey-Bass.

Burns, J. M. (1978). *Leadership.* New York: Harper & Row.

Carpenter, D. S. (1991). Student affairs profession: A developmental perspective. In T. K. Miller & R. B. Winston (Eds.), *Administration and leadership in student affairs: Actualizing student development in higher education* (2nd ed.). Muncie, IN: Accelerated Development.

Cohen, A. M. (1998). *The shaping of American higher education: Emergence and growth on the contemporary system.* San Francisco: Jossey-Bass.

Cuyjet, M. J. (1994). Student government as a provider of student services. In M. C. Terrell & M. J. Cuyjet (Eds.), *Developing Student Government Leaders: New Directions in Student Services, 66,* 73-89.

Downey, K. M. (1981). Majoring in self-interests, minoring in apathy: A challenge for the new activists. In D. A. DeCoster & P. Mable (Eds.), *Understanding Today's Students: New Directions for Student Services, No. 16,* (pp. 77-87). San Francisco: Jossey-Bass.

Ender, S. C. & Carranza, C. (1991). Students as paraprofessionals. In T. K. Miller & R. B. Winston (Eds.), *Administration and leadership in student affairs: Actualizing student development in higher education* (2nd ed.). Muncie, IN: Accelerated Development.

Garland, P. H. (1985).*Serving more than students: A critical need for college student personnel services.* Washington, DC: Association for the Study of Higher Education. (ASHE-ERIC Higher Education Report No. 7)

Garland, P. H. and Grace, T. W. (1993). *New perspectives for student affairs professionals: Evolving realities, responsibilities, and roles.* Washington, DC: George Washington University, School of Education and Human Development. (ASHE-ERIC Higher Education Report No. 7)

Higher Education Research Institute. (1996). *A social change model of leadership development guidebook: Version III.* Los Angeles: University of California.

Horowitz, H. L. (1987). *Campus life: Undergraduate cultures from the end of the eighteenth century to the present.* Chicago: University of Chicago Press.

Howe, N. & Strauss, W. (2000). *Millennials rising: The next great generation.* New York: Vintage.

Kirk, C. M. (1999). Nexus: Campus as place. *Planning for Higher Education, 28,* 39-44.

Klumpyan, T. J. & Langdon, E. A. (2000). Nonhierarchical leadership in action: Creating change on our college campus. In C. L. Outcalt, S. K. Ferris & K. N. MacMahon (Eds.), *Developing nonhierarchical leadership on campus.* Westport, CT: Greenwood Press.

Kotter, J. P. (1996). *Leading change.* Boston: Harvard Business School Press.

Kuh, G. D., Schuh, J. H., & Whitt, E. J. (1991). *Involving colleges: Successful approaches to fostering student learning and development outside the classroom.* San Francisco: Jossey-Bass.

Langdon, E. A., & Mathias, N. B. (2001). Designing experiential training sessions for the social change model of leadership development. In C.

L. Outcalt, S. K. Ferris, & K. N, McMahon (Eds.), *Developing nonhierarchical leadership on campus*. Westport, CT: Greenwood Press.

Levine, A. (1980). *When dreams and heroes died: A portrait of today's college student.* San Francisco: Jossey-Bass.

Levine, A., & Cureton, J. S. (1998). *When hope and fear collide: A portrait of today's college student.* San Francisco: Jossey-Bass.

Light, R. J. (2001). *Making the most of college: Students speak their minds.* Cambridge, MA: Harvard University Press.

Mable, P. & DeCoster, D. A. (1981). The college environment. In D. A. DeCoster & P. Mable (Eds.), *Understanding Today's Students: New Directions for Student Services, No. 16*, (pp. 15-22). San Francisco: Jossey-Bass.

Mangan, K. (2002, May 31). Leading the way in leadership. *The Chronicle of Higher Education, 48*(38), A10-A12.

McMahon, K. N. (2001). An interview with Helen S. Astin. In C. L. Outcalt, S. K. Ferris, & K. N, McMahon (Eds.), *Developing nonhierarchical leadership on campus*. Westport, CT: Greenwood Press.

Miller, T. K. & Jones, J. D. (1981). Out-of-class activities. In A. W. Chickering (Ed.), *The modern American college*. San Francisco: Jossey-Bass.

Morrell, S. A. & Morrell, R. C. (1986). Learning through student activities. In P. S. Breivik (Ed.), *Managing Programs for Learning Outside the Classroom: New Directions for Higher Education, 56*, 77-87.

Mullendore, R. H. (1992). The "joint statement on rights and freedoms of students": Twenty-five years later. In W. A. Bryan & R. H. Mullendore (Eds.), *Rights, Freedoms, and Responsibilities of Students: New Directions for Student Services, No. 59*. San Francisco: Jossey-Bass.

Nuss, E. M. (1996). The development of student affairs. In S. R. Komives & D. B. Woodard, Jr. (Eds.), *Student services: A handbook for the profession* (3rd ed.). Jossey-Bass: San Francisco.

Performa, Inc. Retrieved September 10, 2004, from http://www.performainc.com/xxxxx.html

Roberts, D. C. & Ullom, C. (1989). Student leadership program model. *NASPA Journal, 27 (1)*, 67-70.

Rogers, J. L. (1996). Leadership. In S. R. Komives & D. B. Woodward, Jr. et al. (Eds.), *Student services: A handbook for the profession* (3rd ed.). San Francisco: Jossey-Bass.

Rost, J. (1991). *Leadership for the twenty-first century.* New York: Praeger.

Rudolph, F. (1962). *American college and university: A history.* New York: Alfred A. Knopf.

Schoeder, C. C. & Mable, P. (1994). *Realizing the educational potential of residence halls.* San Francisco: Jossey-Bass.

Schoenberg, R. (1992). Praxis: Broadening the base of leadership. *Liberal Education, 78*(5), 38-53.

Shaw, G. B. (1903). *Man and superman.* Cambridge, MA: The University Press.

Spitzberg, I. J., Jr. & Thorndike, V. V. (1992). *Creating community on college campuses.* New York: State University of New York Press.

Strange, C. C. & Banning, J. H. (2001). *Educating by design: Creating campus learning environments that work.* San Francisco: Jossey-Bass.

Vellala, T. (1988). *New voices: Student activism in the '80s and '90s.* Boston: South End Press.